"You Can't Practice At the Game"

Strategies on Winning at Life, Not Just Surviving in Life

The Art of Mastering YOU

Vol. 1

RJHodgesspeaks LLC
Atlanta, GA

"You Can't Practice At the Game"

Strategies on Winning at Life, Not Just Surviving in Life

The Art of Mastering YOU

Vol. 1

For More Information Address

R.J. Hodges

RJHodgesspeaks, LLC

This book is dedicated to Roy A. Hodges & Carolyn J. Hodges. It is because of both of you that I am inspired to be my best each and every day. The foundation you gave me is why I'm able to still stand strong and excel. I wish you both were here physically to experience this moment with me. However, spiritually I feel your presence all around me every day. I love you both always.

TABLE OF CONTENTS

Introduction

The teacher who is indeed wise does not bid you to enter the house of his wisdom but rather leads you to the threshold of your mind.

~ Khalil Gibran

As you are reading, you should be excited because all the information that graces these pages will be straightforward and easy to relate to.

Don't you hate those super technical books with the huge five syllable words that no one understands? Trust me; that will not be the case here. Listen, this is coming from a guy that took four hours to figure out how to program two numbers in my last cell phone. That alone proves that technical stuff is not my strong suit. So my first goal and priority was to write a book that was extremely clear, effective, and easy to comprehend.

You Can't Practice At the Game is targeted towards a few different types of people.

On one hand, you may be a young adult that is just now entering or exiting college and embarking on your journey to professional success. The experiences that come along with that can bring about a burst of energy fueled with pure excitement, passion, and vigor to accomplish those goals and dreams that have played over and over again in your mind for years. The goal is to learn to properly channel that energy to work for you in order to produce your desired results. When starting on that journey, creating a foundation is everything. The principles contained in these pages are geared toward establishing a solid foundation.

Perhaps you are a middle-aged adult that has been in the workforce for a while and have even started a family, but now you're seeking a bit more out of life than just financial success or fancy titles. You understand what it is like to reach some of your goals, but now realize that maybe you have a different purpose in life that is worth pursuing. This is merely your transition phase, and some of the principles in this book will be exactly what you need in order to properly reinvent yourself and thrive in a way that seems a bit intimidating just because it is unchartered waters. On the other hand, you could be a more mature adult who wants to look at this level of personal development as a refresher of what real success and fulfillment in life is really about in order to professionally achieve. We can all admit that with the responsibilities and challenges life brings, it is easy to lose sight of what really matters. Whoever you are or wherever you may be at this point in your life, this book with the somewhat peculiar and thought-provoking title holds a special message that will speak to you specifically.

By no means are the cleverly crafted words written here meant to give you all the answers to your life. It was not written to tell you that the be-all and end-all lies within these pages. However, it was written to help you learn to discover those answers on your own . . . to get you, the reader, to take a deeper look at yourself. My motive is not for you to agree with me on everything, but to get you to think outside of the box and consider all the different perspectives that are presented. The goal is to help you perfect your strategic mind; to be able to see all angles of every move that you make before you take the step.

In order to see all angles, the mind must be trained to view subject matter from many different perspectives. Something you will notice is that I purposefully provide subject matter that may appear the same on the surface, but consider the underlying point of view in which it is given. I also make it a point to repeat things in several different ways so that the mind is able to gain insight from each idea, and not just merely digest a concept in only one way. When considering the perspective, you will get a different message from something that appears to be the same, but is actually quite different in nature. The strategic mind must learn to see the different dynamics in each situation, and determine which perspective is best fitting for your personal circumstance.

A strategizing mind doesn't merely adopt principles in their basic format, but a carefully cultivated intellect knows how to properly manipulate the principle to cater to specific needs. A strategic thinker will take into consideration several different outcomes before a move is made. Just like a wise chess player carefully plotting where to move next, always keep the thought of winning the game in mind. Once your mind is able to break down life into the smallest details and visualize strategies for conquering situations, it all becomes less challenging. The objective here is not to lead you on the path in which I traveled nor carve out a path and persuade you to follow it. The purpose is to give guidelines, perspectives, and certain principles that will be effective as you carve out a path of your own.

The lecturer and poet Ralph Waldo Emerson chose to say it this way: "Do not go where the path may lead, go instead where there is no path and leave a trail." Wisdom is achieved when an individual finally gets the realization of the knowledge they have, and learns how to apply that knowledge to get the results desired. Not just learning how to apply that knowledge one time to one situation, but learning how to apply that knowledge every day on purpose, and mastering the art of getting favorable results.

Welcome to this journey of mental strategy and critical thought. This writing is devoted to your personal development, your intellect, and how both of those things working together will guide you to places beyond your greatest dreams. If you really open up and become very honest with yourself, this book will show you exactly who you are and where you are in your journey. Then it will highlight the areas that need a little more work in order to perfect the winner in you.

I wrote this book from the standpoint to make you think and plan out your next move. It also acts as a medium to make you consider, ponder, and take into account where you are right now and how to properly move forward. The mind-set you should be in is mentally strategizing your way in or out of any situation.

Never being stuck or in a position where you feel there is no way out.

Volume One of this series was created to help you develop your personal foundation so when it's time to add the professional piece to the puzzle, it fits perfectly. This investment into your personal development will make your professional achievements rather systematic in the sense that the strategic mind will know how to create the proper foundation that professional success must stand on in any given situation. Another important thing to remember as you read is it's not necessarily about the words on each page, but more so about the words you hear in your head and heart as you read. I like to call this the message behind the message. There is a message that will be conveyed to everyone, but then there is a specific message within the message that will only be conveyed to you. Yes, your mind, intuition, and inner thoughts will speak to you. As you go through each chapter, your own thoughts will begin to speak to you about your personal life, your experiences, and things you need to do or pay attention to.

Some of your thoughts will begin to relate to what is being said, and some of your thoughts will have to reason in order to connect to things you have never experienced or contemplated before. Please do not ignore those inner thoughts. It is absolutely vital that those thoughts be written down after each chapter. Please don't wait until later to do this, it must be done immediately after each chapter. Use the page provided at the end of each chapter to quickly write down any thoughts you may have – I don't care how big, small, or abstract those thoughts may be. Even if you believe the thoughts did not relate to the chapter you just read, please write them down anyway.

Take a moment after each chapter to write down what your personal intuitive thoughts were saying to you as you absorbed each line. Those thoughts will be the blueprint to creating your personal strategy to whatever it is that you desire. I know that each and every one of you already holds the answers to your life challenges and desires on the inside of you. I know you were born with everything that you need, every strategy, every skill set to become the greatest "you" possible. However, we all need help at times to remind us that we are great and to help unlock our full potential. The quest to see more of that greatness starts when you begin to first look deep inside yourself.

So dive into this book with an open mind and embrace your specific message. Let go of all of the cares that you have or the cares that may have a hold on you. I thank you for choosing to not practice at the game. Take control of your life, you are the master of your destiny. Oprah Winfrey once said: "It isn't until you come to a spiritual understanding of who you are – not necessarily a religious feeling, but deep down, the spirit within – that you can begin to take control." My intention is that this writing awakens that level of understanding into who you are so that all the control is in your hands.

RJ Hodges

President/Speaker

BORN II WIN, LLC

www.borniiwin.com

www.rjhodgesspeaks.com

SECTION I: WINNERS STRATEGIZE

Chapter 1

You Can't Practice At the Game

"I've always considered myself to be just average talent, and what I have is a ridiculous insane obsessiveness for practice and preparation."

~ Will Smith

You Can't Practice At the Game is a very funny title in my opinion, but it made perfect sense at 7:30 a.m. one Tuesday morning when it popped in my head. The meaning behind the title didn't really come to me until about a week later. I honestly just played around with it and unconsciously said I should write a book and call it, "You can't practice at the game." The weird thing is, the more I said the title over and over again the clearer the meaning got. It's a very simple concept, yet it's something I personally have failed to implement on a consistent basis in my own life. I will even take a chance and say there is a multitude of other people that can claim the exact same thing. The bottom line, when it is game time in any situation you must be ready or suffer the consequences for lack of preparation.

There are millions of examples to prove why at game time there is no room for practice. When the director yells action, if you don't know your lines then you are in big trouble. No time to go read the script at that point, or go over what should already have been committed to memory. Think about a professional athlete, a football player for example. When game day Sunday arrives, if that football player has not had a sufficient amount of practice during the week or is not one hundred percent familiar with all of the plays, it's too late. What about a doctor – is it possible to learn how to perform surgery while the patient is on the operating table? If that doctor has not practiced his craft and/or spent time studying the details of surgery then in the midst of the real thing, he or she and the patient are in serious trouble. I'm being a bit facetious, but hopefully I'm making a point. Spending time in prep mode, mentally strategizing and becoming familiar with the upcoming performance is critical. This example can be applied to any area of our lives. How many times have you waited to do or prepare for something, then all of a sudden a situation occurs and you have limited to no options simply because you waited to practice at the game? I've done that before on more than one occasion.

Today will mark the time where we change our mind-set as far as this is concerned. The ultimate goal for this L.I.F.E (Living In Full Existence) book has one solid message. Be proactive instead of reactive. Make accomplishment and winning something you plan for today. Never sit back and wait for things to happen to you, get out in front, and make things happen for you. You must take an aggressive approach in life, stay laser focused on the things you desire, and never give up on the goals you want to accomplish. Always make sure you are ahead of the curve rather than getting caught behind the curve. Most of the time instead of diligently practicing or preparing for the game, we convince ourselves that we can handle anything that lies ahead simply because we feel we are that good. Please tell me that I'm not the only person that ever said I had something under control and realized when the something showed up that I had absolutely no control. I hope I'm not the only one.

Why not take a more proactive approach? By doing so, you are in a better position to win when the inevitable happens. Simply put, don't wait until the last minute to do what you can prepare for right now. Waiting is a survival mind-set, not the winning mind-set. Always remember, the survival mind-set shouts: "I just want to get by. I just want to make ends meet and do just enough in life." First off, that is a very selfish mind-set to have because it only involves you. The winner's mind-set proclaims: "I will conquer all, I want more than just enough so that my life is not just centered solely around my needs, but I have overflow to bless and empower others."

Further, if you wait, you risk the possibility of it being too late. Almost every issue that an individual faces in life right now could have been solved if practice and preparation was implemented ahead of time. Let's say finances are your particular issue due to the economy not being so great at the moment. What if fifteen years ago you started saving money every single month because you knew that one day anything could happen. We have all heard at one point in our lives that it's a positive thing to save for tomorrow. How many of us really do it? And for those that do, how many of us do it on a consistent basis? Well, if practice and preparing ahead of time mind-set was in place, as a result your financial situation may be a bit easier today with fifteen years' worth of savings set aside. This is definitely not information that we as individuals don't know.

This brings me to one of the most critical conversations I ever had, which lasted only fifteen minutes at 6:00 a.m. in a hot sauna at the gym. I mean how many people expect to get life changing advice from a guy sitting across from you in the sauna. After a rather intense workout, I was sitting in the sauna trying to relax and recuperate. With a towel over my head and ear buds in my ear, it is a fair statement to say that I was pretty focused on myself and my needs, and not paying attention to the older gentleman seated on the other side of the sauna. All of a sudden through the music in my ear buds I hear this gentleman say, "You young guys are lucky, you have all the opportunity in the world and a bit of time on your side also. Too bad, most of you don't have a clue what to do with it or are even seriously trying to find out." This was followed by a rather amusing yet heartfelt laugh. I know you are thinking this was very weird, but think about how I felt at that moment. Can you even imagine my facial expression as I looked up and removed my ear buds? Taking a moment to remove the towel from my head and wiping the sweat that was pouring off of me, everything in me was saying who is this guy and what in the world is he talking about? This is when one of the best conversations that could happen in one of the strangest places ever began. The lighting was so dim that I could barely see this gentleman's face. I kindly asked him to repeat his statement so that I could hear it clearly and he did, laughing again just like the first time. He had one of those laughs that made his chest rumble – the type of laugh that is usually followed by a strong cough. Following that he yells out, "I'm Dave." I replied with my name and he began to give me an explanation for this random statement he had chosen to say to a guy on the other side of the sauna. Dave first started out by asking me a series of questions, such as how old I was, and what I did for a living. As I recall, I was about twenty-four or twenty-five years old at the time. Dave went on to ask me where did I put my money, and if I had at least hit the $100,000 mark in my savings account yet. I felt quite awkward to say the least – this conversation was getting even stranger and furthermore, I had no clue where it was going. For some odd reason, I played along and answered his questions. "My money is in my checking account sir and I also have a little in a savings account. And no, I do not have $100,000 in my savings or checking just yet." He let out another one of those laughs, and said, "So, you really plan on working extremely hard the rest of your life huh?" This time I laughed because how exactly do you answer that question? Dave went on to share with me how he was fifty years old and hadn't actively worked for money since his early thirties. He told me about places I needed to put money to gain maximum interest, and investments that would yield amazing results. It wasn't like I had a pen or pad in the sauna so I had to memorize the things he said. Out of everything he said, it was his parting statement that seemed the most profound. "Everyone is either waiting on something special to happen, or following the wrong plan. They are going to really be upset that they didn't put more thought into their strategy for life. I hope you take my advice young man. Have a good day." In a very low tone I replied, "You have a good day too, sir."

I didn't really know how to feel, but knew some real wisdom had just been shared with me. Not only about finances, but wisdom about life. I went to that gym three to four times a week typically at the same time for the next year, but never saw good old Dave ever again. I often laugh when I think of that story as I now refer to Dave as the angel in the sauna who dropped a jewel on me.

Any logical thinking person reading that particular story can agree with everything that was stated. However, why don't we practice for the game ahead of time more often? I'm drilling that question in over and over so you can truly start to analyze why we tend to do the things we do. Why do we wait until the storm hits before finding the flashlight? I cannot tell you how many times I have watched the news, and they tell you that everyone should have a survivor kit in place with certain items in case of a severe storm or some type of catastrophe. It makes perfect sense to me, yet something has prevented me from actually preparing that kit. It's the way I think, my level of procrastination, and my level of programming that says there will always be time to do that later. It's our excuses for why we don't do a thing that lands us in certain positions in life. If the game (or storm in this case) is played tomorrow, I have a lesser chance of winning because I didn't prepare or practice ahead of time. The concept that I am going on and on about here may not be easy to accept because I admit that it will take a high level of discipline. Entrepreneur Jim Rohn had a great saying: "Discipline is the bridge between goals and accomplishment." I truly agree with that statement. I believe if we all consider thinking this way on a regular basis, understanding all of the benefits involved, then the motivation for the discipline necessary won't be an issue.

If winning is your desire in this game called life, it is imperative that you do everything to put yourself in the position to do so. I'm laughing at myself right now because I've done everything that was the opposite of winning while still expecting to win. Now that my mind has been enlightened to see how we make our lives harder than it has to be, I realize that going through life unprepared equals pure insanity.

The rest of this L.I.F.E. (Living In Full Existence) book will be filled with key principles that anyone can use and apply on a daily basis. Life from the BORN II WIN standpoint is not just about obtaining knowledge; it is learning how to effectively apply that knowledge to your life not later, but right now. It has always been said that knowledge is power, but that is simply NOT true. Knowledge is potential power. This means that unless you know how to apply it to your life on purpose and get the results desired, the information acquired is just taking up space in your brain. Also if you don't take the proper initiative to use what you have learned on purpose beforehand, it will not work for you anyway.

We all have enough knowledge on the inside of us to understand how our lives should be governed, how to plan, how to prepare, and how to strategize, but this book will show you practical ways to apply that knowledge on an everyday basis and get results. Forget about the past because it's never coming back, and stop worrying about the future just hoping it turns out well because that doesn't work either. Yet understand that TODAY is what matters most because today better known as the present is your gift. There is so much power in the NOW. We all must use our gift of today and practice so that we can perform well in the future game.

THE THOUGHT PROCESS:

How much practice or prep time do you spend on the important things?

Chapter 2
Tomorrow Starts Today

"You have to take charge of your life TODAY, in order to see change for TOMORROW."

~ Monique N. Fluker, Vice President of BORN II WIN

It seems like it was just yesterday that I was sitting in an English class during my junior year of high school, only half listening to what my teacher was saying. My mind flashes back to the thought of those small wooden desks with sun glaring through the window and mist in the air from the chalkboard. Yes, chalkboards were popular back then, as if we knew about anything else when I was in high school. This was way before iPads and all the fancy technology of today. I remember daydreaming during most of those lectures about how great life would be when I finally reached adulthood. To be able to live on my own, make my own rules, and have nothing to worry about as far as parents and their regulations seemed like total bliss to me at the time. At the age of sixteen, I had no idea how quickly tomorrow would become today. It was as if I blinked my eyes one single time and all of a sudden I was no longer in high school. In an instant, I was a young man facing what the real world had to offer complete with adult responsibilities. And all of a sudden, my junior year of high school didn't seem so bad anymore. Where did the time go?

Then the famous statement that everyone has recited once upon a time crossed my lips and mind: if only I knew then what I know now. How many of you have ever said that? It's such a true statement because in the moment, you just don't know. The writer Mark Twain said: "Twenty years from now you will be more disappointed by the things that you didn't do than by the ones you did do. So throw off the bowlines. Catch the trade winds in your sails. Explore. Dream. Discover." As I grew up and started to repeat that statement over and over again it finally dawned on me that I better start doing what I know now before ten more years creep by and I'm caught like a broken record singing the same sad song. The reality for me as I grew into a young adult was that every second counts and my days of just daydreaming weren't going to amount to much. There are no do-overs in life; the minute that just passed we can never get back. All this means is that we have to truly learn to maximize every moment. It was time for me to get in gear and learn how to create this blissful life that I daydreamed about oh so often. I must admit that there were a few obstacles and challenges standing in my way. Of course it would be no fun at all if the path was paved with pure gold, right? There just has to be a couple of hurdles and mountains to climb along the way.

There were also a few people that were critical or simply misunderstood who I was as a young man, and that presented issues in my life. All the great pressure one needs in order to produce something phenomenal was present. I'm being sarcastic if you hadn't noticed. However, one quote that I love can always sum up the challenges we all may face. Newscaster David Brinkley says: "A successful man is one who can lay a firm foundation with the bricks others have thrown at him." So I decided to gather of all my bricks in life, including the ones others had thrown and the ones that seem to have appeared out of nowhere, and build something special. What are you currently doing with your bricks?

"Tomorrow starts today" sounds like something you'd read straight out of a Hallmark card, or words of wisdom an old person would whisper in your in ear when you're just a kid. It's quite the cliché statement to say the least. However, when we closely examine that saying, it does make a lot of sense. A lot of different aspects about our future lives are presented to us on a daily basis in our current lives. If you pay attention to what is taking place today and understand that history tends to repeat itself, then it will give you a glimpse into the future. It may not be vitally important today, but through some of our experiences and things that we know, we see at a very early age the possible hurdles that may come our way on this journey called life. However, no one really takes time to map out a solid plan to combat those obstacles. Most of the time, we don't even consider what we would do when a hurdle is presented. As human beings, most of us deal with issues as they arise - I lived the majority of my life thinking that was the only way. Yes, dealing with situations as they occur typically is the most common way of handling things, but usually in the midst of an issue we go into panic/survival mode. Will you overcome? Will you make it through? That solely depends upon how great you are under pressure and what type of resources you have or don't have at that particular time.

Do you really want to leave that up to chance? Would it be considered a better idea to look at different areas of life, examine them, and have a plan in place in order to combat possible future issues today? No, I'm not saying you can prepare for everything; some things truly come out of left field. But wouldn't it be good to be ready, just in case? There are many things about our lives and future success that can be strategized. This book was written to help you establish a thought process that equals winning, not just surviving.

The master strategist always knows the next move to make way before its even time to execute. The principle of thinking things through and plotting ahead of time is not just hoping something great will happen. The purpose is not just going off of instinct in a critical moment, but being well trained and prepared for when that critical moment arises, because it will. I've learned that the typical thing to do in life is procrastinate until it's time to worry. This is simply living from one emergency or unprepared situation to the next. How can you win when you are totally unprepared? The various situations we encounter in this life will automatically train, program, and condition us to survive, but where is the glory in just existing? We learn how to make it from one day to the next, not to win and conquer. While it's definitely commendable to make it from day-to-day, I personally have always known life could be so much more than just getting over one hump after another. It's time for a shift in our programming, a shift in the way we think, and a huge shift in the way we live life. The purpose of this book is to prepare your mind to receive some very special principles and suggestions into the art of mastering you.

Take a moment to consider a few things. Even when a country is not at war, their military is always preparing for what "might" happen. So perhaps nothing ever happens, but wouldn't it be smart or considered intelligent to be prepared anyway? Anyone expecting an event to happen – good or bad – trains and prepares for the outcome in some sort of way. Now the goal is not to create overly worried, hypochondriac type people who are always thinking about worse case scenarios and how every minor detail of life might possibly destroy them. No, that is definitely not the purpose of this book. The purpose is more to get all of us to consider new possibilities and options to win this game called life.

Critical thinking has become a lost art form in today's society. It seems like people would rather follow someone else's game plan expecting the same results rather than learn from that person's pattern and carve out a path of their own. When creating your plan, remember that it should involve the specific steps necessary in order to make sure that it will actually come to fruition.

I want to encourage you to think about tomorrow today, and how we can make tomorrow better by planning today. That is certainly not a foreign concept, and sounds rather simple, right? However, as a society we are taught to plan and prepare for some things, but not for others. It's okay to strategize and prepare for victory in some areas, but other areas are completely omitted. This is a concept that we use, but only apply to a handful of situations. Why is that? Did someone write a rule book stating that you should try to prepare for certain things, but not others? Is it okay to plan and be ready for one type of situation, but neglect another?

It is considered normal and sometimes mandatory to have insurance for certain things: life insurance, homeowner's insurance, or even automobile insurance "just in case" something occurs in the future. Whether you know it or not, that is a strategy for winning. For every person that carries those insurances today, you are indeed preparing for tomorrow. It is an act of putting yourself in the best position to win later down the road when or if something occurs.

So, why stop there? This concept endorses the status quo, but could be so much more beneficial if only applied to more areas in our lives. The same person that will enthusiastically converse with an insurance consultant about one of those services will overlook the fact that they are on their tenth carbonated drink of the day. This is not a great practice for maintaining good health, and not paying attention to the types and amount of food you consume should be considered bad strategy for future good health. Health is, or should be, a part of your winning strategy for life, right? That many carbonated beverages will ultimately put you in a position to fail health wise later in life rather than win. Do you see how the concept of thinking ahead can be beneficial if only applied to more areas of life? Basically, life is a game of thinking and planning; either you will out-think it, or it will out-think you. Making the next move in life is inevitable, but the real question is will that move have a strategy behind it, or not?

On the contrary, it's not typical or normal to have job or career insurance. Meaning no one really prepares for a potential layoff or company restructuring by having a second stream of income in place beforehand. With all of the other things in life to consider, most people leave this option off of their to-do list. In fact some people with so-called "good" jobs snicker and make jokes about the co-worker that does things outside of that job in order to create additional income. So in reality that person with the think ahead mentality is playing it smart, and those with the jokes are living off of a bad plan or even worse, no plan at all.

Back in the 1980's Ronald Reagan once said while on his presidential campaign trail: "Recession is when a neighbor loses his job. Depression is when you lose yours." No one ever thinks it will happen to them, until it does. That is the common mentality in our society. Even though most people show up to work every day in fear of being let go because their position no longer works for the company's bottom line, subconsciously we convince ourselves that it cannot happen to me and neglect formulating a future plan. Those same people would not even participate in their own rescue if you threw them a life raft. Why do we think that way? Why wouldn't we do things to ensure success rather than disaster?

Is there a reason that you keep waiting until it's time to worry? Why wouldn't some level of action or planning on your part be done now?

I have been that person, so I'm speaking from experience. For example, many people are not proactive about their health, even when one knows certain ailments run in the family. How many people take the initiative to plan when they are healthy in order to take an aggressive approach to preventing that same illness in the future? Most of us don't even want to think about the possibility, and there really isn't a standard way that most people handle such things. But I guarantee when the situation arises, most of us will wish we had. Allow your strategic genius to think about ways to ensure that you aren't caught in the same position.

The point I want to make is, why does everyone in the world want more out of life but continue to do what is normal only to get the same results. Why do we desire to be better, but neglect to do the things that better requires? I lived a life of wanting more for years, but there was nothing behind my want but a wish that I would somehow get lucky. Any of you still waiting on luck to knock on your door?

Over the years I've learned that when preparation meets a situation, success is more than likely the outcome versus being unprepared. Based on your life today, how many things do you wish that you had been prepared better for ten to fifteen years ago? How many things will be present in your future life tomorrow that you could get better prepared for today? The key is, don't wait because every moment counts. It's time to take charge of every area of your life and get off the passive "let's wait and see" rowboat. Winning in life is something that must be planned, thought out, and executed. It doesn't just happen by chance or because you have a good idea.

THE THOUGHT PROCESS:

What have you put off until tomorrow that you should have started today?

SECTION II: WINNERS TAKE INITIATIVE

"Success comes from taking the initiative and following up . . . persisting . . . eloquently expressing the depth of your love. What simple action could you take today to produce a new momentum toward success in your life?"

~ Tony Robbins

I still remember my mother, all five feet and four inches of her with the feistiest attitude always telling me, "Don't continue to just talk about it, do it."

Where does all this start? At this point, hopefully the concept is very clear and concise. What we do or don't do today clearly will define our tomorrow. Winning in life is not by chance. People who win in this life do it on purpose because of one very key and vital fact – they took the initiative to make things happen. It matters not where you come from, your social status, or the background that you have. If you take initiative, you can win. People that win take a vested interest in making sure that their success is not left up to chance. It was once said that being casual about life will get you absolutely nowhere. In fact, those who are casual about life usually end up becoming casualties of this life. That simply means that either you take an aggressive approach to control your life, or life will control and potentially destroy you. If you aren't careful, life will take an imaginary rope, wrap it around you, and pull you in whatever direction it desires. The idea here is to take that same imaginary rope off of you, wrap it around life, and then YOU start to do the pulling. It is imperative that you take the initiative and exercise your authority to move your life into whatever successful path you desire.

So, how does one take initiative you may ask? What exactly is initiative? Initiative is defined as the power or ability to begin or to follow through energetically with a plan or task. A beginning or introductory step; an opening move. Notice initiative is about taking a step; it's about being in motion and taking action. Initiative not only thinks, but it also does.

The first step to taking initiative is very simple, and that is to make a quality decision to do so. Right off, I know some of you aren't impressed with that step. It's not mind-blowing and definitely doesn't sound like some mysterious secret that some believe is required in order to take your life to the level desired. Most people feel that by reading this book they have already made a decision to take the initiative. That is not necessarily true. In order to make a quality decision, you must first fully understand exactly what a quality decision is, what it entails, and what corresponding actions are associated with a quality decision in order to make it valid.

Quality decisions are those choices that are made that will produce the results you want. It is a decision that has been well thought out and all possible outcomes of that decision have been considered. I remember working long days at my former job, sitting in traffic, and getting home late feeling extremely tired. See, I knew the next day would be a repeat performance of the same routine, and anything I could do that evening to make getting out of the house on time the next morning easier would be extremely beneficial. Now, guess what my choice was when it came to getting my clothes ready for the next morning versus watching a moving and falling asleep? Yes, I chose to watch the movie and fall asleep on the couch. The next morning I woke up rushing and wishing I had made the decision to prepare better the night before. The fact is, I knew the best decision that would produce the results I desired, but instead chose a different route.

So my bad decision put me in a position to not win on the level I could have had I chosen wisely.

This type of decision making is so important to factor into your life. Saying that you are making a decision to take initiative and practice before the game involves a few things. Whenever a person makes a decision, at the same time that person must create a plan of action to help properly execute that decision. How many times have you made a decision to do or not do something but three months, three weeks, or even three days later you notice that you haven't followed through with the decision made? Why does that happen? It happens because if there was no plan, boundaries, or corresponding action put in place ahead of time, then that decision will more than likely be short-lived. In order to see a decision become a full-blown reality, it's imperative that the proper foundation is in place.

Thinking ahead of time is also a huge part of a viable quality decision, but it's only half of what you need in order to reach your final destination. This brings me to the question, what is the first step going forward? Now remember, a vital component to any accomplishment is action; it's all about what you can do today in order to get the results you want tomorrow.

Throughout the next few chapters, you will find key points to assist you in laying that foundation.

THE THOUGHT PROCESS:

While reading, did anything come to mind that you may need to take initiative on?

Chapter 3

Proper Decision Making

"Many people fail in their career, business, and relationship, and others get stuck because of their inability to make quality decisions."

~ Nkem Mpamah

How does one stick to their decision of taking initiative and practicing before the game?

The belief that a quality decision made from your conscious mind is the open door into the reality that you desire is a very profound statement. That concept is rather logical, wouldn't you agree? What is a decision? By definition, to decide means to settle conclusively all contention or uncertainty. To make up one's mind. To get a better understanding, the root words are CISE and CIDE.

The Root CISE which means CUT and comes from the Latin caedere and caesus. The suffix CIDE which means to KILL is developed from the Latin word meaning CUT, and thus both forms are treated together. So when you look at the word de-cide, you must break that word down to get a full understanding of its meaning.

The prefix de- means away from or removal of. So when a person de-cides, understand its reference is to cut off any uncertainty or any other option that may go against that which you have chosen as the direction that will best assist you in reaching your destination. To break away from any and everything that goes against the choice you have made.

Remove things that don't coincide with the decision. That is something that I believe with every fiber of my being. If you want something in life, decide that it is yours and completely disregard any other options that may say what you decided cannot be achieved. It's necessary to make a decision and then have tunnel vision about making it happen even when outside circumstances seem to say it will never come to pass.

Aaron was a young kid that a friend used to mentor back when I was just learning the ropes about working with youth. I got a phone call one day asking if I wanted to attend a mentoring event similar to a big brother/big sister organization in order to see how it all worked. So my friend Janice, who was a huge advocate for youth and a long time mentor as well, came to pick me up and then told me we had to first go pick up her mentee, Aaron, before heading to the event. I was extremely excited because I love the energy and expectation youth typically have about their future and just life in general.

As we were riding in the car I noticed the direction that Janice was driving in, observing the route and then the exit she took. Being that I was very familiar with the neighborhood I immediately looked at her and asked, "Where exactly are we going?" because we were venturing into an area not considered the safest part of town. Janice quickly replied, "Well, this is where Aaron lives and I come here quite often to pick him up for events. So we arrived at Aaron's apartment complex and we both got out of the car and walked to his building.

When we knocked on the door, a guy that looked to be in his mid-twenties answered and Janice politely said, "Hello, I'm Aaron's mentor and I am here to pick him up for the event today." The guy that came to the door never said a word to either of us, no hello or anything. He just left the front door open, turned on his heels, and as he was walking away yelled out to Aaron. Young

Aaron came running out of a back room excited as he could be and ready to go. Aaron was an eight-year-old boy that was so intelligent and had a plan for his future despite the circumstances he was currently in. As we traveled to the event, he talked and talked about how he planned to be an engineer when he grew up.

At the event, the host asked every kid in attendance from similar environments as Aaron to make a decision that no matter what, they would stay in school and reach their goals. Each kid stood up and made that decision and promised to stick to it. However, I noticed something different in the eyes of young Aaron. It was like he knew exactly what he was committing to, and he meant it. I only got the opportunity to encounter Aaron a few other times after that, and he always said that he "didn't hang around the bad boys in the neighborhood" as he called them. Aaron would tell me that those boys would get him in a lot of trouble if he hung around with them, and that may interfere with him growing up to become an engineer. His ability to focus in on what he wanted out of life and not allow outside circumstances to interfere amazed me.

I didn't know it at the time but Aaron had made a quality decision, and whether he knew it or not had cut off all distractions of anything that could interfere with what he decided. Years went by, probably nine or ten, and I had lost contact with Janice until one day in the grocery store of all places, I spotted her walking down the aisle. We were so happy to see each other, and one of the first things I asked was where young Aaron was and did she still keep in contact with him. When I said his name Janice almost burst into tears she was so shocked I remembered him. She told me that Aaron was all grown up, had received a full academic scholarship, and was in college well on his way to becoming what he said he wanted to be at age eight. I shook my head and somehow I just knew from the moment I met him and the type of decision he made that nothing would hold him back. Aaron used quality decision making to take himself out of a rural inner-city apartment and directly into the path of his dreams.

Now if an eight-year-old can do it, we as adults can use proper decision making to take us wherever we desire to go as well. However, if no one has ever taught you how to properly plan, strategize, and execute that decision, then chances are it will not be long before you backslide on the very thing you decided to do.

To decide to do something opens the door for it to happen. It's a total mental shift. It turns your entire being in that particular direction. However, just because the door is open doesn't mean a person will know how to walk the path successfully. For example, let's say you make a decision to take the initiative where your finances and business success is concerned. By doing so, you are consciously saying that you will pay close attention to this area of your life and put forth maximum effort in creating exactly what you desire concerning finances and business.

So after you do that, then what? What's next after the decision has been made? Honestly, for a long period of time I personally never knew the next step after I made a decision. Do you continue life just knowing you made a decision to change? What will come of just doing that alone?

You will need to construct a solid plan. When it comes to finances or anything else for that matter, you must first plan exactly what you are going to practice on. Maybe it's something simple such as saving $100.00 every time you receive your paycheck. Well a part of that decision is to create the plan, examine your current budget, and figure out if saving that $100.00 is actually possible. Again, a decision is all about the plan, strategy, and execution.

Every decision should have boundaries set up to protect it in order to make sure it really has a chance to live and breathe. Creating the proper environment to make sure your decision has a chance at coming into existence is vital. Think of making a decision as a huge investment that you have to protect so that it can yield the return you desire. If the decision was made to purchase an investment property then surely one of the boundaries to protect that property would include proper insurance, proper maintenance, and even proper security of that investment. Well, decisions concerning life deserve the same principle of boundaries to protect and give them the chance to yield the best return. In order for a plant to grow, the roots need to be taken care of. The plant will need the proper soil, water, and repellant to keep insects from destroying it. A lot of times our decisions are sabotaged by the insects in our lives that show up to destroy. But that's another story for another day. By no means do I have a green thumb, but I do know if those things are not incorporated then that plant won't survive. In other words something has to be done; a foundation has to be in place to ensure the decision turns into a positive success.

So when making the decision to take the initiative where your life is concerned, what is the plan? What type of internal or external boundaries would you place around that decision to ensure it will happen? Once all of this has been figured out, what is the proper corresponding action that needs to be taken to put the entire plan into motion? Think about it. Have you ever heard making a decision broken down into detail like this before? If only I could hear or see some of the ideas that are going through your minds right now. Allow me to help you out by showing you how to come up with a plan, set boundaries, and how to execute the proper corresponding actions.

THE THOUGHT PROCESS:

What decisions have you made recently? Were they quality decisions?

Chapter 4
The Plan

"A goal without a plan is just a wish."
~ Antoine de Saint-Exupéry

This is usually where a decision either flourishes, goes horribly wrong or even worse, is ignored and never realized. Achieving success is all in the planning.

A plan is a detailed outline that one must prepare beforehand in order to accomplish an objective. It's the detailed strategy that will be used to get to the destination desired. If you don't have a plan, then how will you get there? This would be like traveling with no map or GPS and just hoping that you somehow end up in the right place.

So, how does one create a plan? The first step is to examine your decision and make sure it is specific, which is another key aspect of quality decision making. Let me say this again – a decision must be specific, and to the point. The actress Lily Tomlin said: "I always wanted to be somebody, but now I realize I should have been more specific." That is a funny quote but it often reminds me to ask for exactly what I want or risk getting something that might be close to it at best. A specific decision tells you exactly what you want to accomplish with no questions involved.

Next, it's time to figure out what I would call the three main points you must consider before you can start on any journey.

Three Questions to Ask When Creating a Plan

These points are the foundation for designing any plan. They are presented in the form of three separate questions that one must answer in detail before moving forward with not only creating, but also executing a plan. These three questions must be looked at carefully and honestly because the answers will serve as the details and building blocks for your plan.

Okay, at this point your strategic mental juices are flowing and you are zoned in on the proper perspective. Now, let's focus on the actual creation of a plan. For example, let's say it is a plan to start a business.

The first question is: Where Are You Now? It is absolutely necessary to examine what condition, type of situation(s), and state of mind you are currently in before attempting to move forward. Locating yourself requires turning inward, examining the heart, and your way of thinking in order to discover the many things that may compliment or challenge your decision. This will allow one to know how much work it will take in order to reach the goal that has been set.

How do you find where you are in this process? Discovering this means carefully considering a few things, such as the level of knowledge you have, your current physical, mental, and financial position, and your current skill set or lack thereof as it pertains to the goal.

There are a few other areas to factor in when asking the question of "where are you now?" In line with that question, also ask yourself how much knowledge do you have concerning the business you want to start? How much time do you have to dedicate to starting and running a new business? These questions will help to figure out not only where you are, but exactly where you must start.

Consider all the major components of where your life currently is before putting together your plan. Physically you may be working a job that takes up the majority of your time, so that is something to think about when developing a plan. Figuring out when you will be available to work on your goal and implement your plan is very important. Once you answer these questions, then you will know what the beginning steps to accomplishing your plan should be. While answering these questions, if you discover that you don't know much about the business/industry you are going into, then getting that knowledge should be one of the beginning steps. Learning the details about the business you want to start now becomes one of the first priorities on your action plan.

Finances may be another aspect to consider when you think about where you are right now. How much will it take to start a business of this type? What type of budget do you currently have? Will you be dependent upon getting business loans from a bank or investors in order to have money for your up-front expenses? What type of start-up expenses will there be? If you have no clue, then financial research will be another item to include in your action plan.

These first steps help determine where you should start concerning the plan. This is where practice makes perfect because right now I know your strategic mind may be saying this is all so much to consider, but this is what great strategy is all about. During this time, you are exercising your strategic mind because you have to consider all of the angles. This level of prepping, planning, and looking at all of the details is what great strategy consists of.

Thinking in great detail and using mental strategy is not normally taught. So when you first begin to think in-depth on this level, your thoughts are everywhere. It can even be a bit stressful or frustrating to start. But as you go along it becomes easier to see the specifics and break things down so each move that you make is a successful one.

The second question is: Where Exactly Are You Going? Remember, a specific destination is imperative when traveling to the final result of your decision. It's impossible to create an accurate plan if the outcome desired is not exact. Oftentimes, we make abstract decisions and wonder why accomplishing them seems impossible. When there are no specifics involved and your plan lacks vital details, chances are the decision is not measurable and unattainable.

When considering this question, you must allow your strategic mind to think about the end result. What is the ultimate goal for the decision that has been made? Always have an exit strategy in your plan. How far do you want to take this business venture? Is this a venture you want to pursue for the next five to ten years, or is this something you plan to dedicate the rest of your life to? How big do you plan to grow your business? Will your business always be local, or do you plan to expand to different areas? What is the overall purpose for this decision? All of these are questions to consider when thinking about where you are going. The ultimate destination of your vision will play a major role in what type of plan you will need to put in place.

Last but definitely not least is the final question: How Are You Going to Get There? This question involves considering in which direction you will travel, what would be the most intelligent route to take in order to get where you are going, and what things need to be done along the way.

Where are you now? What position are you in? What are you able or not able to do currently to start your business? Have you investigated how others in your business/line of work have succeeded? When starting a plan, knowing how much work will need to be done to reach the goal is imperative. Think about your answers to these questions, and what you must do to get on the right path to achieving your goals.

I used to help a friend out with his landscaping business, and people would call to ask how much the company would charge to landscape their yard. We would let the potential client know that we'd have to first come out and see the yard before quoting a price. Why is that? Because we needed to examine what condition the yard was currently in so that we could determine how much work and time it will take the landscaping crew. Those factors are what determined the price. So finding where you are in your goals will determine how much work and time is needed to accomplish your plan.

Remember this is all preliminary research in order to determine how much work needs to be done.

Based upon where you are and where you want to be, the steps on how you will get there will become your detailed plan. It may start with simple research, learning about different types of business structures, or even creating a solid business plan. There is no such thing as too many details in a plan. As a matter of fact, the more details, the better.

In addition, a plan is not something that goes on forever. A real plan should have a time frame attached to it. That simply means that your plan should have daily, weekly, and monthly goals so that something is accomplished on a regular basis. Once you know where you are and where you are going then the plan allows you to work backwards in a sense. Having a solid end game from the beginning will provide the knowledge needed in order to fill in the middle part of your plan in order to and reach your determined destination.

Finally, when answering the "how will you get there" question, it's very important to understand that the plan must be broken down into specific objectives. Please do not make the mistake of taking a five year plan and trying to accomplish it all in one day. Be sure to break it down into objectives, which are simple steps according to what needs to be done first, second, third, etc. You will then see how much easier it becomes to create strategies in order to accomplish the specific goals set in your overall plan. The first objective should be basic and very simple to accomplish. It could be as easy as finding out how many businesses in your area do the exact same thing you aspire to do.

All of these things could be potential objectives in your overall plan, but each individual objective needs a plan and time frame within itself.

Why are objectives so important to have? If the plan does not have objectives that are simple, attainable steps then most people will become overwhelmed. Have you ever made a big plan but got discouraged because there was so much to do? If your plan seems like it is impossible to accomplish then chances are you will abandon it at some point. Remember, the only way to eat an elephant is one bite at a time. That is the mind-set to have when creating a plan. Consider each objective as yet another bite of that elephant and very soon you will have conquered the entire thing.

THE THOUGHT PROCESS:

Any plans you need to make? Were the plans that came to mind personal or professional?

Chapter 5
Proper Boundaries

"Boundaries aren't all bad. That's why there are walls around mental institutions."

~ Peggy Noonan

What is a boundary? By definition, a boundary is a line that marks the limits of an area; a dividing line. A boundary can also be defined as a limit of a subject or sphere of activity. A boundary represents how far one can go before reaching an area that may be defined as unproductive. Boundary or boundaries can be related to a Latin word Determino which means: to fix the limits of.

Simply put, you must set certain limits around your decision and your plan. The things that will help or hurt you must be identified when carrying out your plan. What specifically should you do or not do daily to ensure the decision and plan will work as desired? First, think about all the things that could possibly hinder your plan. What types of things might prevent the results of this decision from becoming a reality? Think about some of your current life challenges, personal shortcomings, and how they may play a destructive role to your future accomplishment.

After your plan is in place, boundaries must be set in order to give the decision the proper environment to thrive in. Not setting boundaries around your decision is like driving without a seat belt. It's the equivalent of riding a motorcycle on the highway with no helmet. Why would anyone do that? Yes, it may seem okay at the time but definitely lacks the main ingredient that can prevent an epic fail. The boundary is a precaution to make sure the decision will not end badly, and the desired results are achieved. It just doesn't make sense to not have everything needed in order to reach your goal.

One Friday morning I was sitting at my desk working on my laptop when the phone rang. I clearly remember looking at the phone, not recognizing the number and sending it to voice mail because I was a little busy at the time. Also when you don't know who it is, sometimes you feel better just sending it to voice mail. Well, maybe that is just my philosophy. The call came through on my personal cell phone so I didn't think it was a business call. I figured I would just check the voice mail later and return the call. Literally two minutes later my phone rang again and it was the same number. Okay, a pet peeve of mine is never call me more than once back-to-back because that just makes my blood boil. And if you do call me back-to-back it had better be a real emergency. This time however, I answered the phone only to hear a woman's weary voice on the other end.

"RJ, is this RJ? I really need to speak with RJ Hodges," she said, and actually used my full name so that told me this was someone I had to know really well. When I asked her name, she replied,

"This is Angela Turner," and then proceeded to tell me how I knew her.

It turns out that Angela was a friend of a good friend of mine. To be honest, it took me a second to recall who she was because we had only met maybe once or twice before. Angela went on the tell me that my friend referred her to me for coaching and she needed help with a decision she had made, but was unable to make it happen. Angela was a single mother with two young children and her decision was to go back to school in order to create a better life for her and the kids. I first and foremost applauded her effort and ambition. I knew going back to school and being a single mother was a huge step because of the sacrifices that would have to be made. I stopped doing everything I was focused on prior to that call to help Angela identify what was hindering her plan of going back to school. The first thing was to ask her the same questions we just talked about when creating your master plan. Angela had a well thought out plan, and I was pleased to hear that she had really taken time to think about where she was at currently, where she wanted to go, and how she planned on getting there. Going back to school and furthering her education was going to be the vehicle to get a paralegal certification so that Angela could potentially get a job in a law firm where she had a great contact.

The plan was perfect; the problem was this going back to school thing. Angela's biggest hurdle was she already had a full-time job which she needed to keep in order to provide for her family. Working full-time and taking care of the kids seemed like it left no time to go back to school in order to advance. So right then I told Angela that I hoped she had a few minutes because I knew if she would just listen and incorporate what I had to share, it would make a tremendous difference in her life. The first thing I did was ask Angela to describe her daily schedule. This would include everything she did from the moment she opened her eyes until the moment they closed, without leaving out any details.

The one thing I noticed was that even though Angela went to work and took great care of her children, she also spent quite a bit of time with her friends every week, even if it was just them stopping by her house for a couple of hours. Angela was involved in a couple of social organizations with friends that she truly enjoyed. Also based on her responses, Angela was a social media junkie. It is amazing how much time people spend posting or looking at things on their favorite social media sites. In the midst of her describing her days, there were certain questions that I knew to throw in to find out what else she was doing that she might want to purposely leave out. I'm a professional so I can't just rely on her to tell me everything – it's mandatory that

I keep a few tricks up my sleeve. The key here is you have to be honest in order to identify hindrances, and Angela did that.

I went on to explain that having her friends come over, the social organizations, and the social networking sites were becoming enemies to her decision and were roadblocks that would inevitably destroy her plan. Those are very harsh words, but I needed to add some shock value so that she would get my point. The reality was, time was hindering Angela from going back to school and I had just identified a lot of time Angela was spending doing unnecessary things that she could let go of in order to reach her goal. The boundaries she needed to create were letting her friends know there would be no more dropping by until she got her certification; the social organizations may have to do without her for a little while; and definitely restrict her social media time to only one day per week. Angela didn't seem extremely excited about my suggestions, but she knew they had to be done "if" she truly wanted to accomplish her goal.

Putting those boundaries in place would allow her to take an online course in the evenings while still being at home with her kids. Angela was amazed that her issue was so simple to resolve. Something she thought was impossible was literally made possible by just putting some boundaries around her decision in order to make sure her plan would really work. Again, it is important to look at anything that could potentially hinder your plan as an enemy, and treat it as such. The great news is that the boundary you put in place may not last forever, depending on what it is. The last time I spoke with Angela she was only months away from getting her certification and was really sure she would have a job offer as a paralegal as soon as she finished. To this day, I am so proud of her and glad that I answered the phone the second time.

The enemies to your decisions must have proper boundaries to defeat them in order to make your decision a reality. There must be something put in place to counter situations that may present a challenge to you. Let's recap the steps:

1. Make a quality decision concerning your goal. This is all a part of Taking Initiative.
2. Then narrow that decision down to make it extremely specific. Remember, a vague decision is not a specific decision, which will only get you in the vicinity of what you want. A specific destination will get you to the exact location.
3. Create a plan with details and a time frame. Remember the key points to creating a plan. Answer the three questions carefully and honestly in order to help you set a course toward your destination.
4. Outline your plan into specific objectives. It's okay to break your plan down into objectives in the order of importance.
5. Identify any and all hindrances that may stop or prevent the decision from becoming a reality.
6. Set up and enforce boundaries in order to protect your decision, and give it the proper platform to be carried out.

I want to go into more detail about the enemies of a decision. Please allow that phrase to sink into your strategic mind because it will be valuable as you practice and prepare for even more greatness. Why do certain actions pose as enemies to your decision? Why would you think about these things ahead of time? You always want to be prepared with a good plan for potential hindrances because they could stop you from reaching your destination. In essence, thinking about certain barriers ahead of time should be a part of your overall plan to reach the goal. Remember, we are no longer waiting until game time to take action, we are preparing ourselves now. You now have entered into the mind of the skilled chess player who out-thinks his opponent in every move. This is the mind-set of being proactive rather than waiting and having to react. It is an aggressive offensive and defensive approach to winning. Never leave anything to chance in a battle and when it comes to your pursuit of purpose and true happiness this is the most important battle of all.

If you made a decision to go out of town, then you would have to plan according to your destination. If you were going across country, then driving may be an enemy of that decision depending upon your time frame. For example, if your decision is to leave Atlanta, Georgia on Tuesday and you need to be in Los Angeles, California by Wednesday, then driving a car is an enemy to your decision. Why? The fact is there is no way you can drive that distance and make it in your time frame. Boundaries are those things that must be thought about in order to protect a quality decision. In this case a boundary would be that driving is out of the question because the only way you will make it within that time frame would be by taking an immediate flight.

If going back to school and getting an education is your decision, then time may become a possible enemy of that decision. As an adult and the responsibilities that come along with that, time becomes very precious. A boundary that should be considered in making this decision would be proper time management. Think back to Angela's story for just a minute. Perhaps, a good portion of your time is consumed by television and the strong desire to watch all your favorite shows. A worthwhile boundary to combat this may be only watching television once a week. So maybe you will have to record your favorite shows during the week in order to watch them on your one television day. Whatever your boundary may be, if it is not in place and strictly enforced you may find yourself wasting valuable time doing things that are not productive toward your decision and plan.

It could be that as an adult you have friends that will say negative things about you pursuing an education late in life. It is not uncommon for the people you love and care about to be critical of your goals. When people are critical of you making positive changes in your life that is typically a sign that you are starting to make some great advancements in the world. Malcolm X said: "If you have no critics, you'll likely have no success." I say bring on the critics. A boundary to put in place in order to overcome this might include not discussing your endeavors with naysayers. Remember, it's always the small things in life that will hinder you. Seemingly unimportant things that we don't pay attention to usually come back to bite us later.

Some may read this and say it borders the line of being too extreme. In response to that, consider this when attempting to accomplish anything in life. In order to get extraordinary results, one has to be willing to do things that are out of the ordinary. There comes a time in life where pushing yourself to what may seem extreme to others will yield the results others only dream and talk about. I personally live by a quote that motivational speaker and best-selling author Les Brown often says: "You must be willing to do the things today others won't do, in order to have the things tomorrow others won't have." Setting up boundaries around the decisions you make may not be something others would do, but you definitely should.

Another way to identify areas where boundaries need to be put in place is to look at your decision and identify personal flaws that you believe will prevent you from carrying out the plan that has been made. Anything that could potentially be a crack, break, or breach in your plan will need to be addressed. In doing so, something has to be put in place so that it will not sidetrack you. For example, an alcoholic in recovery may recognize that a flaw in his or her plan is the old drinking buddies they use to hang around. A boundary now would be that even though you still love those people, it may not be productive to hang around them while they are drinking alcoholic beverages due to the possible influence it will have on the goal at hand.

Boundaries are not difficult to set up; most of us just will not do it because we think we are strong enough to deal with the hindrances as they come. Again this goes back to the theme of waiting and hoping instead of preparing and winning.

How does one identify a flaw? Since none of us are perfect, stop and think: what is your imperfection? This is an area where honesty and the ability to make sound judgments come into play. The strategic mind that has identified its own weaknesses knows how to make moves so that those weaknesses are properly shielded. This in turn creates a mind that is unable to be taken advantage of.

In my own personal life, I must say that I haven't always been honest with myself concerning my flaws. Especially regarding my many business ventures and the challenges they have presented. With one particular business venture, I remember having a hard time figuring out exactly what was going wrong. I didn't have a great deal of expertise in that line of work, and the best term to describe me at that time was ignorance on fire. That simply means that I was very excited, determined, and passionate about what I was doing, yet I had no clue as to what I was doing. It was an investment venture dealing with stocks and I had no knowledge of the stock market or trading at the time. It's funny now, but it definitely wasn't funny then.

I made a decision to get involved with a group of investors and my main goal was to reach one of the top executive positions within their investment organization. It was a sound decision and at the time I even had somewhat of a plan in place. What was not known is that my personal flaws would show up and cause roadblocks for me on this journey. The first main flaw was that I didn't know this venture would require me to truly look at how I dealt with money. I was ignorant about finances and didn't understand that money was a tool to be used; so instead I let it use me.

The set of friends I involved myself with during those days were not focused on business ownership or anything other than just having fun and exploring life. I must admit that I was not completely focused either, as I actually spent quite a bit of money during that time funding those crazy adventures. Nothing wrong with fun adventures, very typical when you are young and feeling invincible. My flaw was that I spent the majority of my money hanging out with friends, and doing so was in direct conflict with the business I was trying to build. You see, this business venture required me to invest a monthly fee in order to maintain my share of the stocks and investments. I found myself struggling every month to pay my portion of that fee. So after going in circles and bumping into this barrier over and over again, I finally set up a boundary. My boundary became that I could only hang out and spend money with friends once every other month. That may seem a bit intense, but that is the one way I could assure I would have the money for the business and accomplish the goal of my plan. A good boundary that helps to produce a positive result will often take a sacrifice on your part.

Another one of my biggest flaws was procrastination (I know . . . I'm the only person that suffers from this disease!). My boundary for this flaw was that I started making myself do things when they first came to mind. Even if that something wasn't considered urgent or a big deal, it had to be done right then. That boundary was put in place to teach me to develop a habit of not waiting. It literally taught me to be proactive. In essence, it was a mechanism to teach me to practice before the game even before I came up with the concept. So it's mandatory for you to identify any flaws that will hinder your plan, especially where taking the initiative is concerned.

A flaw by definition is a feature that mars perfection. Since none of us are perfect that means we all have flaws. What usually comes up when you try to accomplish a goal? What stops you? What seems to make accomplishing goals difficult for you? The key is to figure out which of your flaws usually keep you from the success you desire. Once they are identified, logical boundaries must be put in place to counteract that flaw. If the proper boundaries are set up and there is a precise plan in place, you are well on your way to reaching your goal.

THE THOUGHT PROCESS:

Are there any hindrances in your life that usually stop you from reaching goals?

Chapter 6

Corresponding Actions

"Every suggested idea produces a corresponding physical reaction. Every idea constantly repeated ends by being engraved upon the brain, provoking the act which corresponds to that idea."

~ Scott Reed

The last ingredient to this taking initiative recipe is definitely one of the most important. The type of action that a person may take when attempting to reach a goal could be detrimental. The only actions that work are corresponding actions. To correspond means to be in agreement or to be similar; equivalent in function, position, or amount. In other words, those are the type of actions best suited for the decision that was made. The level of action must be in harmony with the exact objective of your plan at the time. Please pay very close attention to everything that is said in this chapter, because this will take your strategic thinking to another level.

The moment I first learned about corresponding action was the day I started to get real results in my life.

Corresponding actions can be classified as actions that are not overly extreme for your particular situation at the time, and actions that are not so insignificant that they produce no results. It is actions that will yield the best outcome for where you currently are mentally, physically, spiritually, emotionally, financially, etc. They are actions that will correlate to your goal perfectly. A corresponding action is like the right puzzle piece, perfectly fitting into your present state of being. There will be no need to force a proper corresponding action because it will fit all on its own. These are actions that will aid in accomplishing your ultimate goal, yet fit whatever immediate objective that is currently at hand.

Have you ever made a decision, then acted on it, and later realized that maybe the actions taken were not sufficient or perhaps a bit overboard? If so, as a result of that – what happened? If I had to guess, I would say it probably didn't turn out according to plan. Lest we forget, and as previously discussed, a plan is all about being able to carefully map out the intricate steps and details needed to get you to your ultimate destination.

Proper corresponding action is when things go according to plan because the organized activity to accomplish an objective was thoroughly thought out and executed for that particular step of the process. It is so tempting to try to execute an action that is not planned for your current step of the process. I say this all the time: don't get ahead of yourself in the process. Be sure not to drift too far ahead of the course. If you are too far to the left or right with the action taken, then the results may not come out exactly as desired. The last thing anyone wants to do is go in circles with their plan and see no real results. No worries though, before this chapter is over all the things you need to gauge your actions will be very clear.

Every year on January 1 people make a decision to lose weight, get in shape, or eat healthier. I have also made that decision(s) at the beginning of the year, what about you? Anything regarding health or weight loss can be classified as one of the most popular New Year's resolutions. And these are great decisions; it's taking the initiative where your health is concerned and some people even take the time to create a plan to help them carry out the decision made. However, oftentimes they fail because the corresponding actions are not properly fitting for their current situation. In fact, according to statisticbrain.com only 64% of people that make New Year's resolutions make it past the one month mark of commitment. That number drops drastically to 46% when referencing people that make it past the six month mark of commitment.

For example, a person who has not worked out in years will all of a sudden create this plan to work out five days a week. Perhaps the individual makes it through the first week, but by week two is totally burned out. This choice of action was so extreme and intense that now the individual ends up quitting on the ultimate goal of getting in shape. It's a case of corresponding action gone wrong. Clearly, the level of action taken at the time was not appropriate for that situation. It was an unrealistic goal for what that person was physically able to do at that moment. What might have been a more logical, attainable corresponding action? Well, maybe start off working out two days a week and gradually progressing to five days a week is more realistic for a physical body that has not endured that level of exercise in years. Eventually a five day workout will be the outcome, but may not be the correct level of action at that moment. Starting with two days a week would have allowed the body to get properly acclimated and progress to the more challenging level, slowly permitting the process to reach the ultimate goal of a five day a week workout schedule. In this case, because the proper corresponding action was not implemented, the plan and decision will not be realized. There was simply no harmony, logic, or balance in the initial plan.

It is absolutely okay to take small steps toward your ultimate goal if those steps are progressively getting you closer to the goal at hand. Make no mistake here, it's not that this principle goes against progression, intensity or lofty goals, but puts you in a better overall position to reach the ultimate objective without quitting because of an action that was too extreme to begin with. This will help so that you don't sabotage the plan before it really gets off the ground. It's called development for a reason, which means there is a growth process involved in reaching a goal, and the action taken has to reflect that process also.

Taking initiative, making a decision, and creating a plan of action is not complete if the totality of the results desired are not seen at the end of the process. In order to get there, it's important to gauge which actions realistically and properly fit with where you are in that process. Again, this is practicing before the game, and if you start running at full speed yet neglected the first corresponding action of stretching, then the final goal may be in jeopardy. Everything about winning in life has a lot to do with proper order, organization, and taking progressive steps. No expert starts out as an expert; they spend time practicing so that when the test, game, or whatever opportunity comes along, they are ready and suitably prepared.

Something comes to mind in my own personal life. Some years back I was learning about cleansing the body from toxins and how it is essential for optimum health. It intrigued me to such a degree that my decision was to give it a try. However, along the way I discovered that before a cleanse it was a good idea to let go of a few things in my diet, so I decided to do what is known as a fast. People generally fast in order to rid themselves of something in their lives for a period of time, or it is often used to refrain from a particular thing. Fasting is an act of sacrifice or denying yourself something that you enjoy, but may not be the best thing for you at the time. Some people may fast from certain foods, certain types of activities, etc.

While driving in my car during rush hour traffic, I made a decision to fast from some of the bad food I was consuming at that time. It truly seemed like a great idea. I read all this info about cleansing your system through fasting. My plan was to fast for twenty-one days straight, which is just three weeks. That in essence sounds rather simple when you think about it, or at least it did to me. Okay, don't laugh at me yet, because this bright idea of mine gets even worse. I decided in order to cleanse, purge, or whatever it was I was trying to do to my system, that it would be a good idea to not to eat food at all for those twenty-one days. My plan was to just drink enough water so that dehydration wouldn't set in. In my clever mind, as long as I didn't allow myself to become dehydrated all would be well. I feel like an idiot today because that really makes no sense as far as corresponding action is concerned. At least it made no sense for someone that was a beginner at this, and had never experienced fasting before.

How many people know this may not be a good way for a beginner to start? If you have not come to the conclusion just yet, let's just say that I was in for a real surprise. The reason being, it was not a balanced action for me to take, and I question my level of logic at the time. Now, I'm not a doctor, but to not eat any food and just drink water for a few weeks could be dangerous and damaging to your physical body if you don't know what you're doing. Oh, and let me add that I didn't know what I was doing. A person considering doing something of this nature may want to consult their physician first. At least it may be smart to start slowly and build your way up to this level of fasting.

Well as you know, I didn't consult anyone and in my ignorance, I just went for it. For me personally, this was not a proper corresponding action to the goal at hand. I actually got sick, felt very weak, and had absolutely no energy. Long story short, my actions were a bit extreme for what I wanted to accomplish and I ended up paying the price. The action taken may have been suitable for someone else, but it was not corresponding for me.

Succeeding at your goal is truly about finding the corresponding actions that work for you, not taking actions that worked for someone else and trying to duplicate them in your life. I obviously didn't think this fast all the way through; neither did I properly strategize my moves. In essence I set myself up to not get the best outcome. I didn't make it past the first week and I felt like crap, literally. Needless to say, I aborted the plan altogether and my ultimate goal was not accomplished. Not only was my plan unsuccessful, but the idea of fasting still has a negative connotation in my mind to this day. The sad part is, people make decisions and create plans all the time, but the actions they take don't line up with what they need to do in order to become successful.

What actions are you taking right now toward your goals? Stop and think about them for a second; are they the proper actions you need at this time? Are the actions too extreme, or maybe not extreme enough? If I had just taken the time to logically think and take a balanced action toward my goal, it would have made all the difference - and I would have received a more favorable outcome.

Karen is a bright young woman who is full of ambition and knows where she is going in life. She is well educated, extremely ambitious, and feels it's time to start her own business. Karen contacted my company for business consulting, but thought my plan was a bit too conservative for her, so she decided to do her own thing. Karen made a decision; she created a plan, and then went and borrowed a ridiculous amount of start-up money from a bank for that business. In all actuality some of you may ask, well what's wrong with that? The bad part is Karen made this move before doing any real research on the type of business she was starting. We tried to advise Karen that borrowing that amount of money was not necessary in the beginning, but she already had her mind made up and was determined to take this course of action. If she had just done more research, she would have discovered that the type of business she was starting did not require the up-front costs she assumed it would. She would have learned that she was doing a lot of unnecessary stuff in the beginning that would not bring her a profit. So, Karen made an impulse decision before figuring out how to generate real income for this particular business. Her level of ambition was high, but her winning strategy was low, and that is not how winners play.

All of a sudden, Karen found herself in serious debt with a business that was going absolutely nowhere. It's not that borrowing a large amount of money is wrong per se, it was just not the proper corresponding action to take at the time. But overall, Karen was a victim of practicing bad strategy and a corresponding action that did not fit her situation at that time. To win, it is imperative to make sure you keep your ambition in the proper perspective so that it doesn't turn into ego. Once ambition turns into ego, then things are done to impress and create a good show. To impress, give a great show, and become a master of creating the illusion of success is the survivor mentality. Implementing a proper strategy and doing things the right way will reap the real rewards of profit and success – that is the winner's way.

Notice one thing I keep saying over and over again, "at the time." That phrase is purposely being used for a reason. Timing is everything in life. Many people operate on a level that is way ahead of where they are in the process at the time. It's okay to see the end from the beginning, but the correct process is knowing how to back up and work step-by-step to reach that end result. It's possible to have a vision of a million dollar business, but if you're starting actions include spending money as if the business is already generating a million dollars, that would be premature and could land you stuck in the starting blocks before the race has even begun. Corresponding action is all about what will work for the portion of the process you are currently in.

Have I said that enough to the point where it truly makes sense and will stick with you? This can be a difficult thing to consider but it's worth thinking about. When taking an action, one must consider the state of being they are currently in. That could be physical, mental, and definitely financial. Also a person has to think ahead and consider whether the action will affect their lives in a positive or negative way. By no means am I saying that you should not take action, because action is necessary in all walks of life. However, take action in a way similar to that of a military general before he leads his troops into battle. A general will make sure all possible outcomes have been considered and his troops are well prepared before they embark on their journey.

Let's say hypothetically, someone approaches you with an investment deal and it has always been a goal of yours to find an investment that would yield great returns. After investigating this deal it proves to be extremely risky, and in order to get involved the action will require the risk of your home for collateral to cover up-front financial expenses. Now some people will be over-zealous and do it anyway, and yes, it could all work out. However, the proper corresponding action would be to find another source for collateral without risking ALL you have, or decide that you aren't in the position for this type of investment at the time. I'm definitely not saying don't take risk, but know your risk and be able to calculate if you can handle it if it all goes bad. Always ask yourself, if this goes horribly wrong what position will it leave me in physically, mentally, and financially? Whatever that position may be, will I be able to overcome it?

Think about it this way: you are working with a Toyota budget. To then disregard that fact and go get a Mercedes Benz is a bad corresponding action. It's okay to have a Mercedes Benz mind-set, but physically you are not in a position to operate there just yet. The key word here is yet – the Mercedes Benz will come, but it is up to you to think it through and figure out if that day is today, or in the near future. Ask yourself if you are in a place to bounce back if things don't go as planned. If not, please consider if the action is too extreme at the time. Again, by no means am I saying that you should not take risks in life, but some actions are way above where you are at that moment in time. There are also situations where the level of action is so insignificant that there is no chance of positive results. These are times where you can play it so safe that it will be impossible to get what you desire.

So it's a rainy day and I'm sitting in a Starbucks. My friend, Nick, comes in and starts telling me how he has desperately been looking for a job. His complaint was no one wants to hire him, so I decided to inquire about his goal a little more in-depth. The first thing to figure out is where his level of corresponding action was concerning accomplishing this goal. I remember asking, how many resumes or applications he was sending on a daily basis. I got a very puzzled look from that question, so I simply asked how many resumes he sent on that particular day. "I sent one resume out today," he replied. Right away, it's obvious that there is a huge issue with the level of corresponding action that he was taking. So, I said, "Nick, you live in a major metropolitan city and you're competing with thousands of people looking for work, and the corresponding action you have taken is to send only one resume during the course of an entire day?" That is unacceptable, and the definition of insignificant action that will more than likely not yield the desired results. At bare minimum, Nick needed to be sending out fifteen to twenty resumes every day just to say he had enough out there for the numbers to even possibly work in his favor.

In life, sometimes we are so anxious to get what we want that we do things prematurely. Those actions seem right at the time because we get what we want in the short-term, but logically don't make sense long-term. All the while, we ignore the proper actions that would truly serve our best interests. For example, we often make purchases that don't correspond with where our finances are at the time, sometimes just to impress other people. The famous actor Will Smith said it best: "Too many people spend money they haven't earned to buy things they don't want to impress people they don't like." Isn't that the truth? For some reason we ignore our intellect and thought process when it comes to incurring unnecessary debt. Again, if you don't prepare today then your plan can not come to fruition in the future.

When taking initiative, there is a lot to consider. This requires thinking ahead and definitely implementing a level of planning. Practice will perfect your level of discernment regarding your actions. The more practice, the better your strategic mind will become at only making moves that will yield favorable results. When it comes to corresponding action, it's all about evaluating exactly what you want to accomplish and understanding that just because you don't obtain a goal as quickly as you would like does not mean that you will never accomplish it.

Learning that doing things prematurely usually ends up in disaster is a great lesson as well. Take it from me, success in any area of your life is worth the process it takes in order for you to get there. When something is premature, it's not ready yet which means there will be flaws. What happens if you take a cake out of the oven too soon? It might look great on the outside but usually it's not ready; then you discover the cake is actually mushy in the middle, ending in total disappointment. There are a lot of people in our society who have attained premature success – it always looks good but in reality they took it out of the oven too soon.

The façade of winning pales in comparison to the real thing. It's the proper action that will give you real results instead of things that just look good on the surface. Once you have your plan down, figure out what is possible to do at the time. People always come to me with ideas and tell me about things they aspire to do. My question to them is, "Why aren't you doing it?" The reason why is always something that is not even relevant to where they are in the process anyway. A friend wanted to do some real estate investing, and expressed how his goal was to purchase apartment buildings and strip malls. Having tried this venture myself, I immediately asked, "How much investing have you done so far?" His answer? "None." I was amazed that at this point, he had never even invested in a single family home. Well apartment buildings and strip malls are definitely a great goal, but what is the best corresponding action today? Where do you start? I did not say these things to kill his dream, but to set him up to play a bigger role later. My next question was, "How is your credit?" He had no clue. As I stood there in disbelief, it hit me how we as people don't pay attention to details and doing things from the least to the greatest. Everyone wants to start at the finish line, how insane is that? I once heard that the only people that start out on top are those that are digging graves. The first action in this instance would be to check your credit;

if your credit is not loan worthy then your next goal should be to figure out how to get your credit score up. Then learn about real estate, invest in a single family home, rent it out, and learn how this process works. This is a part of building your wisdom and perfecting your strategy mechanism. Continue to take the necessary steps and before you know it, you will be in position to invest in apartment buildings and strip malls.

What usually happens is people only have a desire to start big, and when they don't accomplish the big goal because they just haven't reached that level yet, they quit altogether. They never quite understand that success is meant to be built over time. That is why practice is so important. If my friend would have just practiced with single family homes, then when the opportunity for an apartment building or strip mall presented itself, he would have been ready to play in the big game. The only people that get instant success are lottery winners and trust fund babies. If you are neither one, then build your success to that grand level by going through the process. Take initiative, have a solid plan, make that plan simple, create boundaries around that plan, and take the corresponding actions necessary to ensure true results.

THE THOUGHT PROCESS:

Do you have a new outlook on what actions would best fit your plan?

SECTION III: WINNERS ARE ALWAYS PREPARED

"The will to win is nothing without the will to prepare."

~ Juma Ikangaa

Preparation for a winner in this life is known as the great "setup for future success. Are you really ready is the question at hand.

What have you done or what are you currently doing to put yourself in the best possible position to WIN tomorrow? What do you spend the majority of your time doing? Is it spent daydreaming about the future? Is it spent wishing something good would happen to you? Or do you have a daily routine that is molding you into the future vision you've mentally had a glimpse of. The definition of preparation is: to make ready beforehand for a specific purpose. What in your life do you need to get prepared for? What needs to be in order today so that tomorrow is made that much easier for you? Think about the ingredients and elements that need to be combined so that the future success you desire in any area of your life is manufactured properly.

Hopefully a level of understanding comes to mind when that word manufacture is used. My goal is to get you the reader to understand that everything in your life, good or bad, has been created or manufactured from something. It has been manufactured from either great preparation and strategic planning or the lack thereof. Nothing just happens. There is a reason for it, even if that reason remains unknown. Where we are today is a result of how we planned yesterday. The question is how do you set yourself up to win now and in the future? What types of things are needed when you prepare? The time has come once again to go and practice for the upcoming game. Are you ready? Let's get into the first requirement for being prepared to win. Whether your goal is personal or professional, the principles that are about to be discussed are absolutely critical.

THE THOUGHT PROCESS:

What steps have you taken to setup and prepare for your future success?

Chapter 7

Thinking is a Lost Art Form

"Have the courage to follow your heart and intuition. They somehow already know what you truly want to become. Everything else is secondary."

~ Steve Jobs

There is an old, somewhat outdated concept in our society today; most people rarely even use it at all anymore. Comedian and actor Milton Berle said it best: "You can lead a man to Congress, but you can't make him think."

I'm partially joking, but sometimes it does seem that way. There is a concept called thinking; some may even call it reasoning or carefully considering a thing prior to acting on it. This art of thinking reflects on a time when people would use their own God given intellect or innate intelligence to solve issues in their lives and create the outcome they desire. Some would even refer to this as critical thinking because it takes time, effort, energy, and patience to consider all of the variables involved, and determine what would be the correct path for the individual to take. Thinking is defined as using thought or rational judgment; intellect or intelligence. The process of using one's mind to consider or reason about something, then determining from which angle to approach or apply that which has been discovered. Looking at all the details of a thing, taking into consideration the outcomes of the choices one may face, and determining which choice will present the best opportunity for the goal at hand. It involves seeing other perspectives in order to broaden one's horizon so that your view is not limited to only one philosophy.

Does this sound like a hard and tedious process? Would you even consider doing it? Most will definitely say yes, but today the majority of us would rather just have someone tell us what to do. It is so much easier to just follow the path of what we see versus taking the time to create and cultivate our own path. We want someone to tell us exactly what to do so that we can easily get what we want. We have no time to explore our own intellect in order to figure out what the best solution is for our particular situation. It's all about getting the magical steps to get you to the next level. By no means am I saying steps are not good, I love logical steps. However, if we aren't careful, some steps will deceive us into thinking there is no real work involved. It puts us in the mind-set that we don't have to think in order to tailor those steps to specifically fit our situation.

There is a book in every store listing the specific steps to whatever outcome one desires. At the same time, if no thought and proper discernment is added to those steps, most people will not get the results promised. Critical thinking is a part of practicing because it involves something called vision beyond sight. Often I'm reminded that we don't see with our eyes, we see through them. That statement simply means that we see with our mind, and the mind is the most powerful thing we will ever own as human beings. How a person chooses to develop their mind will determine if it becomes an asset or a liability. There are people that are physically blind but can still see how to create a masterpiece. The reason is they have perfected practicing the art of thinking, imagining, and creating. Perfecting those things will give you the ability to break down an entire situation before it even happens. That is what I call your mental strategic genius. It's taking time to sit down and carefully analyze the things you have before you, and then sort out all of the puzzle pieces before you start to put them together. Once the pieces are sorted out, you then have to be able to think and envision that puzzle coming together perfectly. In your mind, you must see where all the pieces go. Then you have to realize that just because someone else has a similar looking puzzle that their puzzle is different, and merely copying their moves as they put their pieces together may not be beneficial to your ultimate goal.

Winning is not about duplicating someone else's efforts to the letter with no thought or planning of your own. I'm a true fan of the great martial arts expert Bruce Lee, and he was big on not duplicating. He said: "Always be yourself, express yourself, have faith in yourself, do not go out and look for a successful personality and duplicate it." That means if your plan is to only go out and make a carbon copy of someone else's achievements not factoring in how your situation is different, the results could end in disaster. Learning to truly think for yourself requires a real exercise of the brain. It takes practice in order to be confident enough to act using your own thoughts and intellect. To take all of the things you currently know, add other perspectives to those things, and come up with a masterpiece that will propel you forward is freedom at the highest level. To be able to read books, study great people, and consider their wisdom and techniques yet use your own wisdom on how that information specifically fits your life and situation, is priceless.

To be prepared for anything beyond where you currently are involves not necessarily following the crowd, not doing what may be popular, or even what seems lucrative. The art of thinking involves getting to a point where you trust that small voice on the inside of you. This action truly takes time and one key element: practice. That voice, that notion and feeling screaming at you to go in a particular direction is very important. The only way to ever know if it's right is to try it out. Start off small, but it is imperative that you learn to trust yourself and have confidence in your inner thoughts and your inner knowing.

Ever just had a feeling to do something or not to do something? Most of you know exactly what I'm talking about. Some may call it intuition, some may say it's your instincts, and in a spiritual atmosphere some may even refer to it as the Creator directing your path. Whatever label you want to put on it is fine with me, all I know is when those instincts or that small voice is saying something to you, pay attention. It may be happening right now even as you read, almost like another conversation going on in your head. Remember in the beginning of this book I said that you should always pay attention to the message behind the message. Have you ever missed out on an opportunity and then later said, "Something told me to do that." Have you ever made a huge mistake and was so mad at yourself because you had a feeling beforehand that was not the direction to go in? It happens to all of us. One thing for sure is that our innate intelligence, the winner and wisdom on the inside of us, is always trying to direct us to the best possible outcome. Will you ignore it or learn to trust it? "Follow your instincts. That's where true wisdom manifests itself." -- Oprah Winfrey.

On March 29, 2005 late in the evening, my mentor and I had this brilliant idea to go play tennis. Now for the record, I truly suck at tennis and this night was no different. After proving to myself yet again that becoming a Wimbledon champion was probably not in my future, my mentor and I decided to go grab a bite to eat. Let me set the scene for you so you get a clear picture of what is taking place here.

I'm driving down a pretty busy street, and turned into the parking lot of a restaurant. Just as we are about to get out of the car, I notice that this restaurant seemed a bit crowded so I suggested that we go to another one down the street. No sooner than I made that suggestion, a feeling, an inner thought, my instinct, that voice inside me said NO stay right here at this restaurant and don't go anywhere. Even though I heard it loud and clear, because at that time I had not trained myself to pay attention to it, I just brushed the notion off. Not five minutes later, we drive down the street and we were hit head on by a drunk driver. To this day, it is the worst accident I have ever been in or even witnessed in my life. Thankfully, we both survived. But what if I had paid attention to the feeling, the notion or inclination that warned me to stay where we were in the first place? I relate this to thinking because it goes back to how important it is to truly develop you and learn to pay attention to the champion inside of you that aspires to direct you to the absolute best outcome. For me, that night was a matter of life and death. By not thinking and paying attention to the inner me, I could have easily lost my life in a moment.

Writing this book is like having a flashback. I remember being young and not knowing anything about thinking for myself, which path to take, or which direction was best for me. However, instead of trusting my instincts, trusting that voice inside me, and thinking for myself, I allowed others to think for me. Yes, I did it unconsciously, but still allowed it to happen. Most people will respond, "No one thinks for me," and on the surface it definitely seems that way. That is the same as saying "I'm not influenced by anyone or anything." Yeah, right. We all are influenced by something whether we want to admit it or not. On that same note, sometimes we allow what people say to carry too much weight in our lives, which can also influence the steps that we take. Someone tells you for years how great it will be to become a doctor because after all, there is no greater joy in the world than helping people. Additionally, doctors are usually well respected and paid rather decently in our society. So you hear that over and over again and sooner or later the decision is made to become a doctor, yet in the midst of that journey you discover there is absolutely no passion within you to achieve this goal.

Have you ever been on a path before, and wondered why you were there? It's a worthy path but it has nothing to do with your own thoughts, it's purely someone else's dream?

Here is where your independent thinking comes into play. Most of the time, because we are afraid to think for ourselves we keep pursuing that goal simply because we don't trust our own intellect. We become experts at silencing the voice inside that is telling us to go another way. We are afraid the intuition that is trying to direct us to the path we should take is wrong. The voice from others and lack of practice in trusting your own inner voice is drowning out the obvious feeling that you have to get on another path that better fits you. And yes, those ten steps to success that you read say stick to your path, and that is a true statement, but is it true for you at the time? Have you thought it through to figure out if that principle is one that should be applied to your life at the moment? Thinking is a key to life, and we must start practicing thinking for ourselves, trusting our instincts, and making proper decisions that fit our lives. By doing so, we don't risk waking up one day living a life that we have allowed others to create for us.

So today, what will be the one thing you decide to truly think about? Ask yourself if the thoughts you have are ones you derived for yourself, or is it other people's visions and beliefs that you are afraid to challenge or let go of, even if they are not working for you. By no means is this implying that one should not consider the advice of others. I truly believe in wise counsel, but the key is that we are responsible for making sure that advice is really wise for us and our lives. There will be a lot of great people in your life that will teach, inspire, and help propel you to new levels. But in order to truly be great, you have to learn how to take all of the good deposits you get from this world and allow them to help you mold yourself into a truly successful individual.

Think of the books you read, the knowledge you gain, and the perspectives given to you as simple fuel to plot your path and run your own race. The sad thing is that most people who think they are individuals are just replicas of someone else. The problem with that path is it suffocates your unique greatness. The key word here is unique, because you were born to do something that no one else can do quite like you can. Thinking is definitely a part of being prepared, and the more you think and learn to act on your own well thought out plan, the better you will be at this game called life.

THE THOUGHT PROCESS:

How prepared are you? How much real thought do you give to your daily situations?

Chapter 8

Research / Proper Training / Become Knowledgeable

"Practice is the hardest part of learning, and training is the essence of transformation."

~ Ann Voskamp

How much do you know? How much do you think you know? If you think that you know enough, then chances are you're wrong. Ever heard the phrase, study your craft? How about the expression that says don't go off half-cocked? Well, the theory behind those expressions can't be stressed enough. Whatever you think you know about the goal you want to accomplish or the situation you want to get out of, learn more. Even if you feel you know it all, do you know how to properly apply what you do know? Adapt a mind-set of not going into any situation with just partial knowledge of it.

This stage of practice and development is what is affectionately known as the "dirty work." This is the time when no one will see or notice you. No spotlight will be put on your efforts, and even less recognition will be given in this phase of the process. This is study time, the method where you start to pour information into your brain so that you have knowledge, perspectives, and intelligent thoughts to pull from. Many people say they desire to accomplish something, but have no real clue of the intricate details of that desire or how to get results. Even if you are just preparing to buy a home in the next year, how much do you really know about home ownership? Do you know the different tax advantages that are available as a homeowner? Did you know you must pay property tax in addition to your mortgage? This is all a part of doing diligent research.

To some, it may sound a bit elementary to put emphasis on studying and getting as much information as possible no matter how big or small the goal is. It may even seem like a minute detail that is really not that important. However, I assure you that the quiet time of acquiring the knowledge necessary will prove to be valuable. There should be extensive time spent learning about whatever it is you desire or want to accomplish. Become good at giving yourself the advantage by knowing details that most people would consider unnecessary. Take great pride in being a student of that which you plan to master, overcome, accomplish, or dominate. The average person only knows general information about any subject in their lives. Basically they know what someone else has said about it, or just enough to get by. The strategic planner that thinks about winning and not just surviving always knows more than just what is on the surface. The diligence that it takes to go above normal requirements means just getting by is not an option. If getting by is all that interests you, this is probably the wrong book to be reading in the first place. Anyone can just get by, but the prepared person is meticulous about the details because the goal in their mind is to win. The question has been asked over and over again: why choose to be average if there is an option to be excellent? The prepared person wants to know exactly how a thing works down to the smallest detail.

Once again, think of training as a solider preparing for combat would. I'm a speaker, and for me it's the time I took to train that makes me great at what I do. I spend time studying my craft, going through what I do over and over again. I study the techniques of great speakers that I admire so that I'm constantly improving. I'm always determined to work the flaws out. It's the will and determination to get better and knowing there is always room for growth and improvement that makes the greats who they are. When you train yourself, it develops a behavior that transforms you into the very thing that you aspire to be, and whatever you are training in will soon become second nature. Anyone that has ever been considered great spent considerable time training and conditioning themselves so that their behavior becomes automatic. The performance that one will display tomorrow is based upon the training that happens today.

What is the key ingredient to training? There is no nice way for me to put this, no real cute way for me to say it so I will just tell you what it takes to become great at whatever you desire.

Training requires hard work and diligence. Training is a daily effort that is done over and over until you have developed in that area. Think of training like a bicep muscle; everyone has a bicep muscle, but if you want that muscle to have tone and definition you must develop it through training. Be sure not to leave this step out and include it in preparation mode because a great deal of training is required in order to master anything. By no means am I saying training has to be stressful, because that just depends on your mind-set concerning the concept. My approach to training has always been to think of it as the glue that ensures the finished product is exactly what I have in mind. If I compete in a race, then training or practice is necessary so that at race time I'm not embarrassed due to lack of development to contend on that level. Are you prepared today to compete on the level that you desire? Could you stand alongside the greatest that do what you do, and measure up?

If financial prosperity is the goal and you want to be a millionaire, the question to ask is can you compete on that level or handle that level of financial responsibility? Look at past lottery winners, most of their lives end up being worse after they win. In fact, according to celebritnetworth.com statistics show that roughly 70% of all lottery winners go broke within a few years of receiving their money. The reason why is that they got something they were not properly prepared for. They had no training on what to do with millions of dollars so the lack of preparation destroyed what was supposed to be a blessing. The way to train for receiving millions is to properly learn how to manage, invest, and budget the money that may be present in your bank account right now. Train yourself for millions in the near future by learning how to handle the money you have today.

No matter what the scenario, if not properly trained and prepared for, it may destroy you. The objective is to win, and the saddest thing ever is when someone reaches a level that is supposed to be an accomplishment that ends up causing hurt or harm. There is a reason for going through the process. It's not smart to go to the gym for the first time and try to bench press 450 pounds. It's not that you will never bench press that much weight, but the mind-set has to be what should I do in order to develop and get to that level.

The year was 1998, and I was an overly ambitious young adult with a business and making decent money for my age at the time. I was literally fresh out of high school so that tells you how young I was. Honestly, I was not prepared for the level of responsibility that came along with business ownership. My personal development was not at a point that it could truly sustain professional success. However, that didn't stop me at all. Long story short, the only thing I knew about money was that I wanted a lot of it, and I had already picked out all of the toys I wanted to spend that money on. I was spending money in my head before I had actually earned it. Anyone ever been there before, or am I the only one?

It's funny because today I'm actually thankful that the amount of money I desired at the time was not made before I had the character to handle it. With absolutely no knowledge, no training, and having no plan, all that money would have destroyed me. We see it all the time in our society. The young rookie ball player that just got drafted with the million dollar contract, yet still has the mind-set of a kid about what to do with all that money. Imagine going from literally nothing to being wealthy overnight – it sounds great in theory, but a lot of people in that situation end up hurting themselves, their families, and often end up in a worse position than they were before the money. We hear these stories about people losing fortunes all the time and in some cases they even end up homeless. That couldn't happen to you though, right? We all say that prior to being hit with that type of responsibility. How in the world could someone blow $30 million dollars in two years and end up homeless? Believe it or not, that is fairly easy when you are not prepared to handle that level of responsibility and the issues that come along with it.

Every level of life comes with a test and a graduation. Every level of success and every game you play will have new challenges. No different from school, really. There is no way you can go to fifth grade if you haven't met all the requirements for fourth grade. The same rules apply in everyday life; it's imperative that you train and master the level you are on right now so that you are ready for what is next. Most people spend their lives just repeating the same grade over and over again. They want to take a shortcut and not learn the lesson of the level they are currently working on. Without learning the current lesson and passing that test, there will be no promotion. The level that you are on may seem insignificant to the ultimate goal, but trust me every lesson has a purpose. Not developing the necessary skills for what you desire ahead of time could make the next level a curse rather than a blessing.

Another way to prepare is to acquire a mentor in the area of what your particular goal is. This does not mean to just copy them, but learn why they took the steps they did to get to where they are. So many people neglect this component in their quest to achieve their goal because obtaining a mentor will require humbleness and the willingness to ask for help. A mentor is absolutely priceless. This is simply someone that has already walked the path you are about to embark upon. Why not listen to their expertise and learn from their experiences? There is no guarantee that your journey or experience will be the same, in fact chances are it will be very different. But you can avoid certain hurdles by knowing what to expect. A great deal of mistakes can and will be avoided when you have been trained on what to look out for, and no matter how much you learn you are not equipped to be your own advisor. Being equipped with the knowledge a mentor can provide will do wonders when you encounter the many things that lie ahead.

There is a principle in life that I honestly try to apply to every situation. Since I'm already giving away most of my strategic moves, I might as well give this precious one away too. The principle advises: "Take what is, and make it better." This means once you acquire a mentor, you listen to them and figure out a way to take their level of greatness and make it better. The aim is not to be just like the mentor, the aim is to be better than the mentor. It's often said that there is nothing new under the sun, but the things that seem new are just old ideas and concepts that someone has taken and made better. They have expounded upon those concepts, made them relevant for today, or improved on a particular area where they could clearly see something was missing. Bottom line is, get a mentor ASAP because in life we all need some form of guidance to help us get to the next level. Research the people that may have accomplished something you desire in life, and I promise you at some point they will reference something their coach or mentor taught them. Even in my industry, Anthony Robbins is considered one of the greatest speakers of our time, and he refers to his own mentor, Jim Rohn, very often. So if using a mentor is good enough for Mr. Robbins who has achieved an enormous amount of total life success, why wouldn't it be good enough for me and you?

How do you acquire a mentor? I'm asked this question all the time, and it's a lot easier than you think. First off, what is the goal you want to accomplish? Let's say you're newly engaged and the goal is to get prepared for marriage. The thought is to make sure you and your significant other are ready for what married life will bring. You have read books about the subject, maybe asked a few people, but now it's time to get some hands-on details and perhaps even some advice. To acquire a mentor on marriage, find someone that has been successfully married for a while. It could be a family member, friend, or even someone at your local church. The key is, make sure that person has some sort of credibility when it comes to marriage. That is not to say someone single will not have great insight on marriage, but you want your mentor to be someone that is engaged in the very thing you are about to do. Once you identify that person, contact them and ask to take them to lunch or dinner so that you can ask questions about the subject at hand. This is not the time to hang out; you, my friend, are on a mission. Let them know what your agenda is, and show up with prepared questions and something to write with. This does not have to be a one-time deal; the action of acquiring a mentor should continue until you have connected with the right person and understand how to reach your goals. Understand, you may have more than one mentor in the same particular area of expertise, and that is perfectly okay. There will be some people that will only have the opportunity to share their knowledge with you once or twice. Some may have more time, and be willing to mentor you on a continual basis. In either case, get the information they have, that is what is important here. Remember this is all a part of practice for the upcoming game. Getting prepared to play well will definitely pay off later.

Now, some people have told me that they tried to get a mentor but it just didn't work out for them. To be honest, I never understood that until it hit me that the principle of giving in order to receive is the best advice to fit this scenario. In our quest for success, accomplishment, or escape from a current situation, the focus is all about what we need. While understandable, it is also a very self-centered time in the lives of most people. This just means that in these moments, you are at the center of attention and it is all about what you need to get, not really about what you need to give. I'm telling you that way of thinking must be shifted in order to achieve.

So maybe you have tried to call potential mentors that are doing what you desire to do, or you think they may have some answers to what you are going through. Perhaps you didn't get the response you expected. When searching for a mentor, here is the mind-set I want you to have; if I serve I will ultimately get my needs met because I am meeting the needs of someone else. That sounds absolutely crazy to most people because usually we are just taught survival. The survival mind says I need to get all I can because it's all about taking care of me. Self-preservation is a true survival tactic. The winner's mind says let me open up and give to someone else because if I have a closed hand not only am I not giving, but I'm not in the position to receive, either. In our pursuit for greatness we come across people that we admire and usually ask them to give, give, and give some more to us and never think about what we could contribute to them. The quickest way to find a mentor, someone that will take you under their wing and teach you all they know, is to find someone to serve.

What do I mean by serve? By definition, to serve means to be of assistance to. To serve is to promote someone else's interest or aid them in some type of way. Whose interest are you promoting besides your own?

Let's say you wanted to be a successful barber but know nothing about the industry or even how to start on your journey. First, I definitely say find the best barber in your area, let that person know your goals, and what you want to accomplish. Take that potential mentor to breakfast or lunch and express that it would be an honor for you to serve them so you can learn the craft. Discovering how you can assist that barber and promote their interests should be your focus. It may start with you volunteering to sweep hair up in their shop just so you can aid them in their efforts. At the exact same time you will get to see how the daily operations work, and what it takes to be a barber. Wait, do you mean in order to reach my goal, I may have to sweep up hair or do a small job that isn't glamorous? Yes, that is exactly what I am saying here.

I know a gentleman who started out sweeping up hair in a barber shop while learning all he could about the business, and today he owns several barber shops throughout the city. That time sweeping hair and serving in order to learn was well worth it. The principle here is this; one must properly learn to give before becoming eligible to receive. Luke 6:38 reads: Give, and it will be given to you. A good measure, pressed down, shaken together and running over, will be poured into your lap. For with the measure you use, it will be measured to you." How can we expect to receive if we don't first give? Learn to be faithful and serve that which belongs to someone else, and it will qualify you to have your own. Please don't neglect the opportunity to serve someone that may be in a higher position than you, or someone you look up to. By doing so, doors will open that you could never imagine and the type of mentor you desire will definitely be the result of your giving and not just receiving.

THE THOUGHT PROCESS:

What was the most important thing about this chapter for you?

Chapter 9

Resources / Taking Preliminary Measures

"Happy are those who dream dreams and are ready to pay the price to make them come true."

~ Leon Joseph Cardinal Suenens

This topic is close to my heart because many of us leave this up to chance when we step out to accomplish or overcome something. This is such a vital step in any development process. If I were ever asked what strategy should be considered in the first phase of implementation, this would fall under that category. What I'm about to share with you must be a part of your strategic winner mind-set. There is a phrase called calculate the cost, which simply means have an idea of how much your aspiration will cost beforehand. Nothing is free, and everything has some sort of price attached to it. The price may be a monetary price or it may be a different type of price altogether. Just make sure it is well understood that everything in life will cost you something. The something for nothing mentality must be done away with right now. The key is to know the cost in advance so that a proper decision can be made if whatever it is will be worth that much to you.

I got a job offer once when I was in my mid-twenties, and it was truly a great opportunity. This particular offer most likely would have helped me along the path toward my ultimate goal. However, after meeting with the organization a few times something just didn't feel right to me. Without giving too many of the details because this organization still exists today, I will just say it is a religious organization and I didn't share their beliefs. When I learned that the cost to take advantage of this job opportunity would mean the organization would expect me to conform to their religious belief system, I made the decision that it was not a price I was willing to pay. This organization required anyone working for them to become a part of their faith and practice with them on a regular basis. It also required that I give up my primary residence and move to the property where the organization provided housing for their top level employees. To be honest, that was too much to ask and in my opinion, a bit of a weird request. Since my beliefs were totally different and the requirements were above the price I was willing to pay for this opportunity, I turned the offer down. At the end of the day, I had to calculate the cost and realized that it wasn't worth it for me.

It's so important to know where you draw the line and where your standards are. In the attempt to become professionally successful or reach the next level, some of us will neglect standards and end up paying prices that will ruin our lives later. Everything that comes to you in the form of an opportunity may look good, but calculate the cost first and decide if it is truly worth it.

What are you willing to give up in order to succeed? What will you have to give in to? What sort of personal or professional compromises will you have to make? All of these things are considered a cost. If paying a certain cost will mean only winning for the moment, then that situation may not be worth it. It's almost like walking into a mall and seeing your favorite sneakers for sale. The sneakers cost $150.00 and you only have $200.00. Guess what? You have a huge decision to make. Are those sneakers really worth the price? Is spending more than half the money you have on sneakers really a beneficial decision to make at the time? Further, what about those opportunities where it's obvious that you will have to do something slightly dishonest or possibly deceive people in order to succeed? Do you do it because it seems like it will benefit you? On the road to obtaining success and becoming great, there will be a lot of "opportunities" thrown your way. The strategic mind knows not to just jump on something that sounds good. Take time to think it through and weigh the pros and cons of what it may cost you. These are all things to consider before moving forward.

Calculating the cost is also relevant when stepping into your plan. What price will you have to pay in order to execute each objective of the plan? This brings me to the question that everyone must ask while in pursuit of a goal: What are my resources? What do I currently have, and how can I use that to get ahead? What or who do I currently have access to?

The French moralist and essayist Marquis de Vauvenargues described it this way: "The greatest achievement of the human spirit is to live up to one's opportunities and make the most of one's resources." This is the strategic process of making a winning move versus a move that will only position you for short-term success, and then it's over. The goal is long-term sustainable success in all areas of your life. Realize that the resources you currently have will help a great deal. Allow me to explain exactly what I mean by resources.

Resources are the things around you that can be used for effective operations. Those things could be money, materials, people, or anything else that would be considered an asset. At this point everyone should know how to create a plan, and the details that are involved in doing so. Now within that plan you can factor in the resources that you currently have available to you. My goal has always been to be an entrepreneur and empower other people to reach their full potential in life. In my pursuit, I noticed an entrepreneur in my circle that was doing the exact same thing I was aspiring to do. Not only could this be a potential mentor, but I had to train myself to recognize that this was a valuable resource sitting right in front of me. This was a resource that had to be factored into my overall plan.

Do you know how many people have resources right within their reach but never truly take advantage of them? It might be as close as a family member or a longtime friend. How many people today are struggling with a goal or searching for ways to get out of a situation, and the answer or resource is right under their nose? It may even be in your own household. Sometimes the people you are most familiar with are those you overlook as a resource. The typical thing to do is to overlook a brother, a cousin, a neighbor, or a spouse because you know them so well. Also please consider that the answer or the exact resource you are looking for may not come from a direct contact you currently have. However, ask yourself this question: who do my direct contacts know that could be valuable to me? I could give countless examples where I took one resource and did what I refer to as "tap root" through them to find the specific resource that I needed. Tap rooting just means being able to not only tap the resources of that one person, but going through them in order to tap into the resources of the people they know as well. Everyone you know knows someone that you don't. It's a beautiful concept for accessing information and saving time in the process.

For instance, I had a good friend that was a teacher at a local school. My objective was to get a project approved by that school district's superintendent. Now I didn't know the superintendent, but what did I have in my resources that would help? I used my available resource by placing a call to my friend the teacher, whom I call Sister Betty. I told her about my project and asked if she would be willing to introduce me to her principal. Sister Betty didn't know the superintendent of the school district personally so that was not a resource of hers. But the resource she did have was Principal Patterson, who was a good friend of hers and they were members of the same sorority. So Sister Betty introduced me to Principal Patterson and said all types of wonderful things about me. I got a meeting with Principal Patterson and told her about my project, and guess what Principal Patterson did? She picked up the phone and called Superintendent Johnson, who was willing to meet with me, hear about my project, and eventually gave the approval I was seeking. How about that for tap rooting and using what I had to get to where I needed to go! Many people would still be making cold calls to the superintendent's office trying to get a meeting. Those blind sales calls may work sometimes, but more than likely it will be more beneficial to look at your internal resources and find a connection.

Once you identify your goal, then the main question is what do you need in order to achieve and win? Once you figure out what you need, take an assessment of the current resources that are available. Who do you talk to everyday? What do they do for a living? Who do they know? What organizations do they belong to? What connections do they have that are a direct match to something you need to move along in the process?

By the way, I will continue to remind you about corresponding actions throughout this book. What if no resources are available for the particular task at hand? I know some of you are thinking about that, so let's address this question. Even if that is the case, still take the time to list the resources needed to get you to the destination desired. It is always better to see exactly what is needed clearly written out so that a conscious plan can be made to obtain those things. At that point it is time to be creative and come up with ideas in order to obtain those resources. Now, please don't forget our lesson on corresponding action.

Oftentimes, I find people feel they need things that truly aren't necessary at the time. Let's say you are in debt and the goal is to get prepared so that eventually you will be able to live a debt free life. Well, some people would say that they need $100,000 as far as resources to clear their current debt. While that amount of money might be the total debt, it may be more appropriate to start with the smallest debt and pay that one off first. The situation may not require more money coming in, yet it may require a budget so that the available monies can be properly used to start paying off those debts one at a time. Instead of looking for a money resource, a proper financial plan or someone that can assist with creating some financial structure would be a better resource to search for. Who do you know that is a financial planner, or may know someone who is?

Whatever you do, please don't allow what is perceived as a lack of resources to stop you from starting your plan. The worst thing in the world to do is to wait until you have everything lined up properly before getting start. Here is a clue – things may never look one-hundred percent perfect to you, but the answer to that is to start anyway. I love the saying "God cannot steer a parked car," which simply means you need to be moving in order to get direction. Even your GPS will not start to talk until the vehicle is in motion. Do the things you can until you are at a point to do the things that may not be in reach today. As you begin to move in the direction of your goal, it is amazing how the resources you need will start to appear and materialize.

Resources will inevitably become a main focus when executing a plan. Many people concentrate on resources because they feel they lack the necessary things to reach their goal or overcome the situation they are in. You may feel you don't have the right finances, knowledge, ability, or whatever you consider vital to reach the goal. The majority of the time, that is just not true. The resources you currently have whether they are minimal or plentiful are just that, tools to be used. The objective is developing the strategic mind to use whatever you have to your advantage. Just because the tools around you are not the same as the next guy does not mean you won't be successful. Resources have to become a mind-set because a truly successful individual can find and use almost anything within their grasp. Truly sit down and think about it, analyze what you have, and let that strategic genius on the inside of you go to work. Please don't be afraid to test the resources you have. Start talking to the people you already know, find out what and who they know. If the level of determination is there, then nothing will stand in your way.

It's similar to the mind-set of the guy that is determined to get in shape but resource wise he doesn't have the money to join some fancy gym. Most people would just stop at that point and do nothing because they feel what is needed and not present or unavailable to them is a hindrance. On the other hand, the determined mind will use anything that will serve as a workout. They will do triceps squats using a living room chair, bicep curls using gallon water containers, or even push-ups with a younger sibling on their backs. That is extremely creative, right? And creativity is definitely what it takes when it comes to utilizing your resources. The determination to make the impossible possible is the outlook one has to have.

In practice for the main event, it becomes a matter of perspective. How do you see a thing? How you see it will be how you handle it. If you see it as a hurdle that cannot be overcome, then you will treat it as such. However, if you see it as a minor issue that has solutions, you will simply move past it with ease. By using that mind-set, everything you have will be seen as a resource and yet another tool to be used to push you to the next level.

The message is, pay attention to resources and use everything around you. Take the preliminary measures needed to know exactly what is required to reach the destination. Just be sure to understand that nothing regarding your situation is a limitation unless you allow it to be. I am a huge fan of the great singer and musician Stevie Wonder simply because his music was always playing in my household as a kid. Here is a man that is physically blind, but refused to allow that to become a limitation. He figured out a way to use another resource which was his hearing, and created musical masterpieces for the world to enjoy. Stevie in his own words told us to use all the resources we have. He simply instructed: "Ya gots to work with what you gots to work with." In other words, use what you got to get what you want because everything and anything if used properly is a resource for your good.

Please have no fear about being creative, because it's the mind that thinks outside of the realm of average that becomes the above average person in our society. Just because no one else would do it the way you are thinking about does not mean it is wrong. It indeed may be the innovative idea that will revolutionize everything around you and create a new level of normal. Normal is only considered normal because someone created it in an abnormal state of mind and people bought into it and made it popular. Think about that as you analyze all the things we have in the world today, and research to find out if it was normal during the first introduction of that thing. Just imagine how abnormal it was when the Wright brothers were talking about creating an airplane. To create a flying object that would transport people through the air. To the people in their day, this was insane and definitely out of the ordinary. Thankfully, that didn't stop the Wright brothers, they kept going and today what was once abnormal is a very normal thing. Someone took their resources to another level, used their strategic thinking, and created a masterpiece. In fact, flying in a plane to your destination is the fastest, most preferred way of travel today. What if they had allowed their lack of resources to stop them? What if they had allowed what people thought about their idea to make them quit? Where would we be today? So to you the reader, I say keep practicing, aspiring, and pursuing with no fear because the future world is depending on you.

THE THOUGHT PROCESS:

Did any resources that you currently have come to mind? List them!

SECTION IV: WINNERS STAY AHEAD AND ARE NEVER LEFT BEHIND

"In life, lots of people know what to do, but few people actually do what they know. Knowing is not enough! You must take action."

~ Anthony Robbins

A winner will never spend their time wishing and waiting. Instead, a winner spends the majority of their time moving and doing. As I take a deep breath, this is definitely a subject I know all too well. I was a victim of the waiting for something miraculous to just happen to me syndrome. It is a very easy cycle to get caught up in. Even though believing and envisioning is something I highly recommend, it does come a time where all out massive action is required. Please do not perceive this section the wrong way. It is important to read this section using your inner vision, and let your mental wisdom speak to you. The way you see yourself, your outcome, and your circumstances will all play a major role in what takes place in your life. To not develop vision beyond sight in your quest to becoming better is a tragedy. However, once that level of vision and belief is there, it is now time to work. A vision shows a person the end from the beginning. Being able to see that develops a hope inside of you, and provides the blueprint for what you are working towards. The key thing in that statement is what you will be "working" for. Not what you will be "waiting" for.

There is no secret that becoming great and achieving anything in this life takes practice and hard work. Now I don't say that to stress you out or give the impression of some difficult journey that is impossible to conquer. The purpose is to give you a reality check that something has to be done in order for something to happen. A great NFL football player does not become great just by watching film of other great players alone. If that were the case then I would be an NFL superstar. Do you know how much time I have spent watching football and studying great players over the years? Then again, that is all I have done in that area - just watched. While watching film has it place, the real future NFL player has to get out and participate in the corresponding action - the physical practice that it will require to achieve on that level. The mind-set again is taking the lead in what you want to happen. Oftentimes we wait until someone is available to help us or to steer us in the right direction. If no one is there to hold our hands, it is common to do nothing. I truly believe in mentors as has been stated in the previous section, but at the end of the day your life, your success, or the lack thereof is all your responsibility.

Get going, start moving, or risk being left behind is what I tell most people I have the opportunity to coach or speak to. If there seems to be no way, make one. By all means don't sit back and think that something will automatically happen just because. This system of life just doesn't work that way. Get up, get out there, and do something toward the goals you have set.

THE THOUGHT PROCESS:

What are you doing to keep from being left behind?

Chapter 10

Get Off the Sideline and Get in the Game!

"Vision is not enough; it must be combined with venture. It is not enough to stare up the steps, we must step up the stairs."

~ Vaclav Havel

To be ahead of the curve requires a certain perspective, an outside of the box way of thinking on how to properly govern your activity. It involves getting off the sideline of life and really getting into the game. That statement has been said before and if you're anything like me I'm sure your question is, "What the hell does that really mean?" How do you even know if you're in the game, on the sidelines, or on the playing field at all? When a person attempts to become greater and prepare for tomorrow it is easy to get caught up in things that are helpful but not necessarily productive.

Back in 2005 I had a mentor that truly opened my eyes and sort of hurt my feelings at the same time. Be careful what you ask for when asking your mentor for advice – most are very blunt and don't have time to sugarcoat things. Of course I had to learn that the hard way. My goal was to build an additional stream of income while working a full-time job. Anyone ever tried that? It can definitely be a challenge, but well worth the effort.

As always, I was extremely excited about the possibilities. If for some reason you haven't figured it out by now, I'm a pretty optimistic type of person. It wasn't much but I had a small extra room that I turned into a home office. Please don't make it seem like I'm the only person that has ever had this bright idea before. You know that tiny spare bedroom that you are determined to make look like a Fortune 500 corner office with a New York City view. Well, perhaps that part was just my vision at the moment. I did everything possible to make it nice and ready to do business in. It was my decision to paint the room a bright color because bright colors are supposedly associated with being vibrant and upbeat. No office is complete without the proper desk setup and the computer to go along with it. At that point, it was time for a trip to Office Depot to make sure I got a desk that would match the décor in my new home office. This business ownership stuff is really serious, because you have to set everything up just right is what I was thinking in my head. Finally, I got the right desk, the right motivational quotes on my wall, and literally a ton of supplies because you can't have an office without office supplies, right? Everything was almost ready to go; just waiting for my fancy new chair to be shipped to me. All of this setup, including painting the office myself, took a good month to arrange. One day my mentor called to ask how I was doing with my goals and what type of income I had created so far. "Well, I haven't made any income yet, but I have reached pretty much all of my goals," I replied. He let out this sigh of frustration before proceeding to ask exactly what goals had I accomplished. I told him about the nice shade of yellow I had painted my home office, and how perfect everything looked. I went on and on about office supplies and how my new chair would be coming in really soon. Finally he interrupted me and said, "Ummmm . . . those are a lot of great activities, but they don't mean a damn thing for real production. You got a great setup, but you did nothing for the business itself."

Yeah, it's okay to say that those comments took me by surprise. I was in shock to say the least, because in my eyes I was being very productive. That Saturday, I learned a harsh lesson on the difference between productivity and just plain old activity, and just being busy without actually accomplishing anything.

Anybody else know the difference? How many of you are in that phase right now? I like to call it the picture perfect let's get it all together phase. Once the setup is complete and you have all your computer gadgets and office supplies lined up perfectly, then what do you do? Ask yourself, how much have you really done for the actual business? That was the main question my mentor posed to me that day. He went on to explain that business was done when something was sold and a profit was made. Everything else while necessary was just good activity. This is a perfect example of things that are helpful versus things that are productive. Oh yes, it is possible to confuse being busy and being productive. The truth of the matter is most people spend the majority of their lives on the sidelines doing things that can be helpful and even necessary, but never really getting in the game and doing the productive things that yield real results.

Ask yourself, am I just busy for no reason? Am I getting any results from what I am currently doing? It is easy to look like success; it's another thing to actually obtain it. Is what you're doing producing tangible results, or are you still stuck on the initial setup and calling it productivity? Perhaps you are stuck in the phase where you are doing too much at once and nothing is happening. A lot of times, we put five percent of our efforts into 100 different things at one time. Yes, you truly have a lot going on when operating like that but usually it doesn't amount to much. Focusing and giving a one hundred percent effort to something specific while making sure you are doing what is necessary for real results is vital. We have to discontinue the mind-set of being a jack of all trades, yet a master of none.

Hopefully I hit a nerve because that was the goal - to jerk you out of the mundane and get you out on the field. Now, don't allow this to make you feel bad if you are indeed stuck in this phase, because I was there at one point myself. Well to be honest, I was there more than one time. It took me awhile to truly learn and master the difference between what is and what is not productive. Again please understand this in its proper context because there is nothing wrong with being prepared, but at some point you have to actually do what you have been preparing for.

The biggest deception is to confuse your preparation time with actual production time. They both go hand in hand, but it is easy to get caught up in one and not give that same type of attention to the other. The moral is, don't get bogged down in just plain old "busy work." This is how people get left behind and never even realize it. Can you imagine how many people had social media ideas such as a Twitter or Facebook but never acted on them? Somewhere ten years or so ago someone was thinking about doing a social network and probably had the perfect lay out to do it. The problem is they are still laying stuff out and have yet to take action. Meanwhile, Mark Zuckerberg, Jack Dorsey, Evan Williams, Biz Stone, and Noah Glass have reached the top of the Forbes list and created fortunes from social media in a short period of time. The mentality of one day I will do, or let me lay out everything perfectly before I do versus taking all out massive action can be quite costly.

THE THOUGHT PROCESS:

Have you ever been busy, but not productive?

Chapter 11

Not Later, RIGHT NOW!

"Past is experience, Present is experiment and Future is expectation. Use your experience in your experiments to achieve your expectations."

~ Unknown

Take a look at a calendar, a watch, a clock, or anything that will tell you exactly what year, month, day, and time it is. At this very moment, right now, today at this very second is what you currently have to work with. Yes, we plan for the future and yes we practice for the future game, but everything starts where you are today. There is so much power in the now because now is when you have the opportunity to make tomorrow better. Here is a slight clue; tomorrow doesn't get better just by wishing it will be better. I will continue to make that point just so it is ringing in your ears over and over again. Tomorrow gets better by doing something today that will put you in a better place tomorrow. How do you take advantage of the power of now?

The first way to take advantage of now is to break the habit of thinking you can do it later. There is no such thing as later or in a few minutes, or when you feel like it. That is just a deception to make you think that time is actually on your side. The reality is that time is always against you until you learn to manipulate time and see it from a different perspective. Can you manage time? Can you learn to use time to your advantage? Yes you can, but the reality is that the moment you are breathing right now is the only moment you are promised, and that is simply because you are in that moment. My question to you, how are you spending each moment of your life? It's a very burdensome question, but just think about it. Did you just waste three hours playing video games or text messaging a friend about absolutely nothing? Maybe you just spent an entire hour on Facebook or Twitter. Now I know I just touched a nerve because most of you are addicted to one form of these simple pleasures that we all tend to enjoy. The question is, do you enjoy these things a bit too much? Do you spend time doing these things and then making excuses for why you aren't productive? I hear people all the time talking about how much time they don't have to do the things they really want to do. If you are indeed one of those people, you will not like the rest of this chapter. I can almost promise you that. This chapter is meant to expose how much time we waste doing things that will not be productive for tomorrow. Don't get scared now, you have come this far. Hang around for a while and keep reading, because I promise there is light at the end of this tunnel.

At this point it sounds like all work and no play and since I know that would truly make for a dull life, here is a solution to the question of how to take advantage of the now and still have some time left over for the simple pleasures like reality television. Please don't pretend like you don't spend time watching those shows because I know you do. That was a joke by the way, lighten up a little!

There is a way to enjoy life and still be productive. Those wonderful television shows draw us in, and don't you (almost) just hate it when they air a marathon. I personally have watched Law and Order SUV for hours during a marathon. Now that would not be so bad if I had prioritized my time and was already done with the more important things that were necessary to push me to where I want to be. I want you to focus on this phrase: prioritizing your time. It's not that we don't have enough time to do all the things we want to do, both productive and miscellaneous, we just use our time wastefully. There should never be a day when your social network goofing off time comes before your study time or before something you were supposed to do concerning your plan to get to the next level of life. So the big question at hand is how do you prioritize your time properly, but still enjoy the guilty pleasures of life? The only way to do that is to incorporate the "two O's" in your life. The two O's are known as: order and organization.

One way to create order and organization is to make a to-do list every single night before bed. Yes, that is my magical advice. Well, it's really not magic at all, but it works if you really do it. This is not a suggestion, but a requirement. I'm sure everyone has heard of this little technique before, but how many of you have actually done it? If you have, how consistent have you been at doing it?

The next question is, do you know how to make a to-do list that is effective? Do you know how to properly organize your day? Just scribbling a few things you may want to do on a piece of paper or saving a few tasks in your smartphone is not quite what I'm referring to here.

The statement, "If you don't plan to win, you plan to fail," is absolutely true. Think about it; people wake up every single day saying they want to conquer the world, yet have no clue what they are doing on that day to make it happen. How do you conquer anything if you don't even have objectives set for the day? We have all been taught to have the right attitude and to be determined, but without a specific blueprint to build off of how far can we go? That is the exact equivalent of saying I'm going to bake the best cake in the world, but have no recipe, not even sure what type of cake you will make, and none of the ingredients in order to get started. Good luck on that cake being the greatest ever.

How in the world will you make something happen if you aren't ready? It's called wasting time because hours will go by and you will be doing nothing, because your accomplishments don't have a daily plan attached to them. Let's say that today is Monday, what is your plan for Monday? Okay, I'll wait in case you need to figure it out. I'm still waiting; do you have a plan for today yet?

Here is something I adopted a while ago, and I still live by it. In order to have a successful year, you must first master having successful months. If you want to have successful months, then you have to learn to have successful weeks. Finally, in order to have successful weeks, you must master the art of having successful days.

For those overachievers that are saying yes you silly little author I do have a plan for today, to you I say, congratulations! Now, is that plan written down? Is it visible? I once read in the Bible, Habakkuk 2:2 "Write the vision and make it plain." And that statement has always stuck with me. Does your plan for today merely exist in your head? If so, that is a start, but we still have work to do. If your plan is just a bunch of random ideas in your head, then it actually lessens the chance that any or all of it will be accomplished in a timely manner. A real daily plan is one that is thought out, written down, and each task is given a sense of priority. The one thing I can promise you, this action really works. Even though it may sound like a hassle right now, just trust me on this because you will be singing my praises later.

I sound overly confident, huh? My challenge to you the reader is to do this for two weeks and see how much it changes your life and the time you have in any given day. Push yourself not to allow any days for two weeks to be left to chance. In other words don't let a day pass where you don't have a specific agenda for what must happen that day. Develop this as a habit, and it will change your life. Author Charles E. Hummel said: "We realize our dilemma goes deeper than shortage of time; it is basically a problem of priorities. We confess, we have left undone those things that ought to have done; and we have done those things which we ought not to have done."

Here is an example of planning out a day:

Random thoughts of things that need to be done on Monday 8/13/2012

- Write a chapter for my book.
- Conference call with my business partner re: promotional video shoot.
- Schedule a haircut.
- Pick up clothes from the cleaners.
- Reply to four e-mail inquiries re: business.
- Get an oil change for my car.
- Read two chapters from my Napoleon Hill book.
- Return two important phone calls.
- Call my sister.
- Attend business meeting.

There is nothing wrong with starting out with random thoughts on your to-do list. At this point, it's about getting everything down on paper. The next step is to set times to your list.

This is your prioritizing tactic. What on this list is the most urgent? What has to be done first, second, etc.? This will require you to look at your overall day and figure out what task can be done around the same time because they may be in the same area. Remember to use great strategy, like a wise chess player. The goal is to maximize your time and be creative with the time you have. For example I would schedule my car oil change and picking up my clothes from the cleaners around the same time because they are within blocks of each other. It would make no sense to get my oil changed and not get my clothes from the cleaners because

I can almost see the cleaners from the oil change business. This alone teaches you to use time to your advantage.

Think about similarities between each task and other things that may make them a match to be grouped together. Also think about what tasks will take longer than others and which ones can be accomplished quickly. By doing so, it will put you in the position to plan accordingly. For example, I would do my best to schedule a haircut appointment early in the morning or around midday. Why? Because I know that my barber is usually super busy in the evening since that is when everyone gets off of work, and they all want a haircut before they head home. Well, I don't want to be in that chaos, so in order to use my time wisely I prioritize accordingly.

Again, think about all the idle time we have that we don't use to our advantage. Each one of my tasks will require me to be in the car driving for a certain period of time. Well there is no point just being in the car doing nothing. What on my list could I accomplish while driving to tackle another task? Calling my sister definitely could be accomplished. This is simple, using my Bluetooth for safety, I can call my sister while I'm on the way to get an oil change or pick up my clothes from the cleaners. Imagine how much can be accomplished in one day if you only have a plan. Also, if this applies to you, learn to delegate some of your tasks accordingly. If you have an assistant or someone that shares similar responsibilities with you, then figure out how some things can be delegated so that it saves you time.

Things that need to be done on Monday 8/13/2012 (Prioritized List)

- 9:30 a.m. – Call my sister while on the way to get a haircut.
- 9:45 a.m. – Haircut.
- 10:45 a.m. – Return two important phone calls while driving to get my oil changed.
- 11:15 a.m. – Get an oil change.

- 11:25 a.m. – Brief conference call with business partner in the waiting room while getting an oil change (this is usually possible because at this time of the morning, no one is in the waiting room).
- 12:00 p.m. – Pick up clothes from cleaners.
- 12:30 p.m. – Reply to four e-mail inquiries re: business.
- 1:00 p.m. – Read two chapters of my Napoleon Hill book.
- 1:45 p.m. – Write a chapter for my book.
- 3:45 p.m. – Attend business meeting.

Just look at how much time is left in the day after I do everything on my prioritized to-do list. Let's say my meeting lasts until 4:45 p.m. At that point I am already done with everything productive for that day. I have an entire evening to either add additional productive stuff or since its Monday I can relax and catch a Monday night football game. At the end of the day, I'm happy, goals have been met, and because I had a solid plan for that day I have taken full advantage of the NOW. My order and organization has put my life in a manageable, well accomplished, and peaceful state.

But wait! What if a person works a full-time job that takes about eight hours out of each day? I know someone is thinking this, so let me share. Is it possible for a person working full-time to still implement all they need to do by prioritizing? Let me answer that question from about eleven years' worth of experience working a full-time job in corporate America.

First of all you have to understand that anything is possible and everything is achievable if you are willing and you know how to do it. First and foremost have confidence that it can be done. The great activist Marcus Garvey told us, "With confidence, you have won before you have started." To answer that question, YES you too with a full-time job and other responsibilities can plan your day with a purpose in mind and maximize the time you have. Now here is a harsh reality, because a great deal of your time will be taken due to work constraints, some of your time in the evening will have to be dedicated to being productive toward your goals. Truth be told, a lot of your evening may have to be dedicated toward your goals. It is possible that you may have to miss a few social events, even a football game, or a couple of hours of sleep. Okay guys stop looking like that; it's not the end of the world. We live in a world of modern technology, so just record the game and watch it when you do have an available moment. The truth of the matter is, everyone you are watching on television is actually handling their business and being productive. Chances are, if they are on television they are creating income and pushing toward some sort of goal, while the couch potato is watching and complaining about how they hope things will change.

The point is, you may have slightly less leisure time but the reward will be well worth it. Is it possible to prioritize your leisure time, work your full-time job, and still reach other goals? The answer is being extremely organized with the time you do have, and being what I like to call "time creative." This just means that you learn to cherish and maximize each and every moment of the day. Once you change your mind-set to seeing each moment as a potential opportunity to accomplish something productive, time will begin to work for you rather than against you. That means examining all of your idle time and taking advantage of those once wasted moments.

What about that fifteen minute break you take in the morning at work? The break where you just get a cup of coffee or chat it up with a co-worker could be used for something productive. When time is already tight, that fifteen minutes could be an opportunity to accomplish a task on your daily plan. Most people get an hour lunch break; does it really take you a whole hour to eat? Even if it does, if time is your issue, figure out a way to be productive while you eat. Some people are saying well, an hour goes by really quickly; by the time you go buy food and sit down to eat it, the hour is almost over. My suggestion? Don't go out to buy food. Bring food from home, that way you already have lunch at your disposal. Here is how I used to create additional time - I would bring my lunch to work and since I ate at my desk, I could still diligently work on knocking out goals on my daily list of things to do. This is definitely an alternative way of thinking when it comes to accomplishing goals in an already busy day. And while this may not sound ideal, when you desire to win anything is possible.

Allow your mind to be creative, and you will discover all sorts of gaps in your day where a few minutes or so could be used in a more productive way. The biggest test is to find the time and not continue to make excuses as to why you don't have any time. Even the moments we spend focusing on how much time we don't have are wasted and could be put to better use. I'm not saying it will be easy and in no way am I making light of working a full-time job, taking care of home, or any other responsibilities. Yes, any or all of these tasks will make reaching your goal more challenging, but not impossible.

There are countless amounts of people throughout history that have taken a complex situation and created something no one would have expected. That is what true success is all about. Think of a little girl born in rural Mississippi with all odds against her. Molested as a child and pregnant by the age of fourteen - that is definitely not the hand anyone wants to be dealt. Now you may be saying to yourself, wow, my situation isn't that bad. Well, that little girl with everything against her went on to become the great Oprah Winfrey we know today. When you look at it from that perspective, your full-time job and difficult time constraints seem minor in comparison to what some people have faced and turned into incredible success stories. Success isn't necessarily given to anyone, but those that truly crave it learn to create it against all odds. So, don't let time or the lack thereof stop you from doing all you are destined to accomplish. The biggest way to prevent this lies in one profound statement, "Never allow your reasons to accomplish now become the excuses that hold you back from reaching your goals." That is my own personal quote, came up with it all by myself because it used to apply to me.

So, what is meant by that quote? Sometimes I find that the very reason why a person wants to accomplish something tends to become the very excuse for why they say they can't realize that particular thing. Let's say you classify the place you work at as a dead end job. It's just a vehicle you use to stay afloat; something to keep the bills paid and a roof over your head. Everyone at one point in life has worked a job like that; I know I have a few times. So the plan to free yourself from this job is your dream to become an entrepreneur and start a business that will fulfill your passion and put some good income in your bank account. Now here comes the dilemma - most people that are working a job to just get the bills paid will not have the luxury to quit that job right away in order to start the dream business. For those in that position, it's imperative that you become two separate people. Now the juggling between being the employee by day to keep the lights on and the striving entrepreneur by evening in to late night to become something you have only dreamed about begins. Whew, I know all too well what it means to become two different people in order to reach a goal.

The thing to watch out for is this: most people will take the very reason to start a business which is to one day be in a position to walk away from that dead-end job, and now make it the very excuse for why they can't build their business. They say things like I don't have enough time, my job takes up all my time during the day, etc. I would stay up later and work on my business plan, but I have to get up early to go to work in the morning. The very reason for living your dream is now becoming your excuse for why you say you can't make it happen.

Please be sure to fight and guard against this way of thinking. Again this is not in any way saying this will be a simple task, but it is attainable if you truly want to go to the next level. For me, I used to just tell myself that I only had two choices: either fight through the challenges and make it happen, or remain the same. That alone would always push me to make yet another step forward, because remaining the same was never an option. So here are a few things to incorporate into your life if you plan to take advantage of the power of now.

1. Plan out your day the night before. Please don't wait until the morning because now that day has already started, and the clock is ticking. Set a time for each task. Remember if you don't plan to win, then yeah, you know the rest, right?

2. Change your mind-set when it comes to time. Learn to take advantage of every single moment. View each moment as an opportunity to get something done. That thirty minute commute to and from work can now become productive time. Get that book you have been trying to read on audio and listen to that during your commute time. No point in wasting time listening to radio gossip and commercials.

3. Instead of making excuses, tell yourself this is just a small challenge that I will find a solution for. You will be amazed what will happen after you train yourself to think this way. Everything will just become an issue that you are about to find a solution for. Solution orientated thinking is much better than worrying and only seeing the problem.

THE THOUGHT PROCESS:

Have you ever put something off until later that can be done right now?

Chapter 12

Never Stop Trying

"Stick to a task, 'til it sticks to you. Beginners are many, finishers are few." Anonymous, as quoted in Small and Simple Things."

~ Marjorie Pay Hinckley

There is a battlefield with a war going on and even though most will not classify it as that, the fight can be judged on that scale. This is the internal fight in your mind between believing in yourself and doubting if the next step will lead to your demise. Even those that deny they have this internal battle can identify with conflicting thoughts to the vision of success you deserve and desire. It takes a lot of constant, consistent, personal development to learn to believe in yourself, especially when outside circumstances convey to you the opposite of what you're yearning for. Activist and author Lydia M. Child said, "Belief in oneself is one of the most important bricks in building any successful venture." However, we all have moments when we become the biggest skeptics in the world and have a bit of doubt about everything. What if I do this and it doesn't work? What if I fail? What if this happens or that happens? Yes, I too have been the "what-if" worrywart once upon a time. To be honest, it still happens to this day in certain situations. That is truly why personal development is a lifelong, ongoing journey.

The best piece of advice is something that the Nike Corporation figured out a long time ago, JUST DO IT! No matter how it feels or even what it may look like at the time, keep pushing toward your goal. Never stop, just keep pressing forward. Anytime you step outside of your comfort zone, expect it to be just that, uncomfortable. However, most of the things we reach for in life will be located outside of the realm of comfort. Here is the one thing I can assure you - if you continue to do what you have always done, you will ultimately get what you have always had. Getting to the next level of your life will require a bit of stretching. Doubt, the hesitation to believe, or the uncertainty in what you desire shows up in order to get you to accept fear. In other words, fear is the beginning of creating a belief system in the thing you don't want to happen.

Fear and faith are the exact opposite of each other. Faith is the substance of things hoped for, the belief in beneficial, positive occurrences happening in your life. Fear is the substance of things dreaded, the belief in harmful, unfortunate, or negative occurrences happening in your life. Belief in either one gives it power to open the door and create the reality of that conviction. Once you accept the fear, it permits what you don't want to happen to enter your life. I once read that fear is having faith that things won't work out. In order to get rid of the doubt and not accept the fear takes reprogramming yourself to only believe the best. Learning to believe the best, eliminate doubt, and erase the fear will take consistency and diligence. Doing things such as adopting affirmations, reading positive uplifting material, and training your mind to believe the best can and does work. This way of thinking cannot be done just one time, it should become routine. It must be done over and over again until it is not just something you do, but something you have become to the point where your belief system automatically accepts only the things you want, and rejects the things you don't want. I will not allow a day to go by that I don't wake up and speak out loud the things I desire, things that I am believing for, and am thankful for. By doing so, I am constantly and consistently training my belief system to eliminate doubt in those areas.

Practice is called that for a reason, because it is meant to be systematic. It is something you do-over and over again until you get it right. The biggest thing to remember is don't look for a miracle overnight, because chances are the miracle mentality will take you out of practice mode and leave you stuck. So many people want a quick fix instead of adopting a new way of living that will produce lasting results. Anything great takes time, and it's okay to grow into perfection. When you step outside of the comfort zone and it doesn't look and feel like what you want right away, people think something is wrong. Also the first time you go to practice it's not always fun or very rewarding. There are times when practice will be strenuous and tedious. It is the process of conditioning yourself to reach a certain level. The purpose of it all is to perfect something that is needed when the time comes to display what you have been working on. The opportunity to display what you have worked on and practiced will always come. The question is, will you be ready? So set your mind in advance to keep going forward no matter how it feels. Have a real commitment to the process long after the level of excitement in which you decided to practice is gone.

In the city that I grew up in, the marching band is a big deal. I started playing my instrument - the alto saxophone - in the fourth grade and figured I was well on my way to one day being a marching band member. I laugh now, but back then that was such a huge goal of mine. I grew up going to football games, envying the marching band, and saying one day, I will be one of those guys. What I didn't know was all the time spent from fourth grade until high school was my practice mode. It was simply just the beginning of getting me prepared for what was to come. I remember going to high school and signing up for the marching band, it was exciting and I knew it would take a lot of work. In my heart, I was ready and figured I wouldn't need much practice because after all, I had been playing my saxophone for a while and in my opinion I was already an expert. It seemed to me that my practice time was over. Little did I know this would prove to be something totally different than anything I had ever experienced. What I did know already would prove to be just enough to get me started with this challenge. Although, in my mind I felt the challenge would be minor for someone like me because I thought that I was more than prepared.

However, no one truly prepared me for that first day of band camp – it was a nightmare to say the least. Imagine spending an eight-hour day in late August in the Georgia heat on a football field, marching, playing an instrument, and doing push-ups when you slightly broke the rules. I was a little more defiant back then so I slightly broke the rules occasionally. After day one, I literally wanted to quit because nothing about it seemed glorious at all. This was definitely not what I had pictured in my head due to one simple fact – it was uncomfortable. For some odd reason I went back the following day and fought through all the discomfort and pain once again. Even though it was never easy, the practice and preparation to my surprise was all worth it. The first time I stepped on a field to perform with the marching band to a sold out stadium cheering us on is unexplainable. Those days of practice when I felt like giving up seemed rather blissful in hindsight as I enjoyed the moment when it all paid off. The reward for my diligence far outweighed the pain of the process.

My thought today is, what if I would have quit just because it was not comfortable or it was hard in the beginning? What if I had quit because it didn't turn out the way I planned after a few practices? Had I quit, I would have never known that amazing feeling of accomplishment after the process. So take it from me, don't focus on how long or difficult the process may be, just keep thinking how sweet the victory will be once the goal is obtained. It is impossible to know real victory if you give up, cave in, and quit. However, the usual reaction if the first attempt at trying something new doesn't turn out great is something must be wrong. Maybe this is not for me after all. Ever had that thought? The most common response is to quit after things don't necessarily turn out according to plan.

If you have quit on yourself in the past, make up your mind right now that this is not an option anymore. Repeat after me: "Quitting is NOT an option." You never know how close you are to your breakthrough. What if the breakthrough and the very reward you are seeking is only one week away, and you quit just before a life changing experience occurs. That would truly be tragic. I once heard well established businessman and former presidential candidate Ross Perot say, "Most people give up just when they're about to achieve success. They quit on the one yard line. They give up at the last minute of the game one foot from a winning touchdown." Please don't allow yourself to be that person.

Life is about the process, and the one thing you should never do during the process is stop trying. In other words, that means never stop doing, never stop taking action, never stop going for greatness, and never stop practicing to become great. Always make sure you are in prep mode for something because it will keep you sharp when game time arrives. Remember what I said in the beginning: when preparation meets opportunity, success is more than likely the outcome. Trust and believe that opportunities for success will always come, but if you are not ready for the opportunity when it shows up, it will pass you by. As you continue the process, just know that there will be a defining moment that will come in the form of a favorable opportunity that will either push you ahead or reveal the fact that you haven't been diligent in your preparation. Maybe for you it's not a huge business goal that is the desire of your heart, you may just want to be more in shape or have a better relationship with a spouse or significant other. Whatever the case may be, know that now is the time to start because tomorrow depends on the now. The mentality to have is continuing to work day in and day out to achieve the vision that is before you. The focus should be how can I be successful right now rather than how can I be successful the following day. Daily accomplishments will soon equal the ultimate goal. Learn to win each day because doing so is the setup to winning forever.

Perseverance is defined as steady persistence in a course of action, a purpose, a state, etc., especially in spite of difficulties, obstacles, or discouragement. Pay very close attention to the last part of that statement. I promise you that as you keep practicing and pressing forward, there will be some difficulties, obstacles, or discouragements. This is not meant to put a damper on your current level of excitement; it is to prepare you so that when those feelings/thoughts come, it's not a shock. The instinct, the drive, the enthusiasm, the knowing that it's possible to be better and do better is the main focal point. That focus will get you through the tough times. Things may not always go one-hundred percent according to plan but don't be afraid to regroup, rethink, and go at it again. When the plan veers slightly off course, learn the lesson quickly and get back on course as soon as possible. There is a true tragedy in not continuing to press on, and pressing on must be done no matter what challenge presents itself. The important thing is that you learn something with each new trial. When you are constantly experiencing the same difficulties and obstacles, that is when it is time to stop and figure out what is it about this lesson you are not learning. Being able to persevere is a trait that is necessary for any level of success.

During the building process toward your goal, it often doesn't look like the outcome you are hoping for. In fact, there are times during the building process where victory doesn't seem to be anywhere in sight. Seeing the victory ahead can be a very tricky thing when you are in practice mode and working on something. Sight would indicate that the only results you will get are those things you can physically see at the moment. Just remember that what you can see is temporary and subject to change. A person can physically see that their car is dirty, but that is subject to change pending you wash it in order to modify what is being presented. So what you see with your senses can be altered, which means it does not have to remain that way.

However, the positive thoughts and images that you envision are eternal. Well, what is the difference between vision and sight? So glad you asked that question! Sight is something that most have because of nature since it is one of the five senses we are granted. That simply means your physical eyes have the ability to process light stimuli and physically comprehend the things that are right in front of them at the time. Sight only gives you the present state of what is there; it doesn't process anything beyond that moment in time. However, to develop vision gives a whole new insight into living and winning. Vision is when you can see a thing even when your eyes are closed. Vision has the ability to process not only what is, but what is to come. One definition of vision goes like this: an experience in which a person, thing, or event appears vividly or credibly to the mind, although not actually physically present. So, vision can process and comprehend unseen things before they physically manifest.

One experience I had with vision was living in apartment after apartment and hating it due to not having any control over my living space. I couldn't make a certain amount of noise or have the type of pets I wanted. Every time the lease was up, somehow they would want to raise the rent. I truly felt restricted and wanted nothing more than to own a home. For a while all I had was sight on the situation (what I can physically see and what I know in that moment). Well, what I could see and what I knew at that time was that I didn't make enough money to buy a home, my credit was not the best, and to top it all off I also didn't have much money saved for a down payment. Even though all of that was true, only focusing on what I could physically see was not helping me get to where I wanted to be. I needed to develop vision in order to see past my physical circumstances and persevere until I reached my goal. If sight is not pushing you ahead, then switch over to vision and start to create what you really desire.

So I did what I had been taught to do by my mentors and books I have read. I started to develop my vision every single day by making home ownership more real in my mind than the apartment situation I was in at that time. The goal was to make home ownership so real to me mentally and visually that no matter what I could physically see, all I could fathom was home ownership. I would go look at homes every weekend to the point where I started to see myself living in a house versus the apartment. If there were open houses in new neighborhoods, it was a must that I attend every open house I could find. All the publications that could be collected about buying a home littered my apartment. It got to such a point that I would cut out pictures of homes and tape them on my apartment walls just to keep the thought of home ownership at the forefront of my mind at all times. I would drive to work in the morning and talk to myself and speak affirmations that I will own my own home, and it will be effortless to do so. Yes, I did say talk to myself out loud while driving. It sounds crazy now, but I didn't have time to care about what anyone else thought; I was in practice mode because I wanted my house. I did it to such a point that my vision overcame my sight. It is on purpose that the last statement is repeated again, my vision soon overcame my sight. It was at such a high level that I would tell people that I'm about to purchase a home and not in a joking way – I was one-hundred percent serious and convinced it was about to happen. When the images in your mind begin to dominate what your physical eyes can see to such a point that it becomes more real than your circumstances, watch out. At that point the impossible is about to become possible!

Now physically, I still had no money and my credit was not that great, but somehow because I could now see it clearly in my mind I knew the direction to get there would come. I was no longer paying attention to what I could see physically in that moment – it was all about that vision of having a home. When I closed my eyes and was unable to see anything physically, I could still see clearly with my vision. I use to imagine myself moving into my new home, to the point where I could literally smell the newness of the house.

A valuable lesson was taught to me during those times. That lesson is simply this: "You don't see with your eyes, you see through them." Everything you see, you see through your mind's eye. Your mind is where your vision is. If you develop that vision then it will eventually overcome your sight. Once that happens, perseverance becomes easy because you are no longer frustrated by what you currently see physically since what you see mentally is fueling your fire. To this day, I'm convinced that because I trained my mind to think that way, innovative thoughts and ideas came to direct me to buying that home. All of a sudden I got ideas about how to create more income, ideas on where to go to help improve my credit, and last but not least, this vision moved me into a path to meet the real estate agent that would bring it all together. There is a force that will work on your behalf when you can envision a thing. There is a door that will open when you truly believe in what you desire. That force will create, rearrange, and setup things to help you bring the vision into existence. I relate it to planting a seed in the ground. Once the seed is planted, the ground starts the germination process to help that seed grow into what is locked inside of the seed. Once you get that seed of vision in you, the force of nature will take over to assist in making sure that seed grows. It will literally unlock what you see and bring it into existence.

I know some of you may say that won't work and it's hard to even believe what I'm saying, but I dare you to try it. I dare you to start focusing more on what you want versus what you don't want. I dare you to stop focusing on what you don't currently have, and start only envisioning the aspirations you have in your heart. I challenge you to stop speaking and saying how bad your situation is or talking about the issues and start talking about the solutions to those issues. Anyone can wallow in and only see the issue, that's beginner stuff. That is simply the survivor mentality way of doing things. It takes true determination and grit to talk about, focus on, and envision the solution.

Not too long after I trained my vision to overcome my sight something great happened – I moved into my first home. Not only did I move into my first home, but it wasn't even a starter home. That vision moved me into a four bedroom home with two and one-half baths. An almost 3,000 square foot home came into existence from what I could see in my mind. Not bad for a guy who initially didn't know how to make it happen. I was still in my twenties at the time and totally amazed because I now knew how to practice and overcome the difficult times. Once you get a breakthrough after practicing, your life will never be the same.

All this happens for the person who says at the beginning that no matter what I'm determined to reach my destination. There will be some bumps in the road along the way, but there is no reason that you should ever stop moving toward the goal you desire. Life and winning requires a certain level of tenacity, which means having the courage to hold on to what you want out of life even during the tough times. It is all possible once you set your mind to stubborn mode that no matter how hard life may push, you are willing to push back ten times harder in order to reach your own level of greatness.

THE THOUGHT PROCESS:

Have you developed your vision for what you want?
What things usually tempt you to stop trying?

SECTION V: WINNERS ARE CONSISTENTLY CONSISTENT

"Perfection of effort is not required, by the way. It is the consistency of attempting to work these tools that brings the progress. It's like anything else. If I want to tone muscle, lifting a ten-pound weight a few times every day will move me toward my goal much quicker than hoisting a fifty-pound barbell once a week. Yes, it really is true: "Slow and steady wins the race." Just try a little, every day. You'll see."

~ Holly Mosier

Doing something one time may get you some results. Doing something twice may get you better results. But doing something consistently will get you GREAT results.

This is a trait that is often hard to come by because it will require a routine. Consistency is the adherence to the same or similar course of action on a daily basis. Doing something long after the mood in which you decided to do it in is gone. Now let's be honest, we don't always feel like doing what needs to be done every single day. In fact, there are days where we put things off until the next day or even the day after that. If you won't admit that, I will because there are days when I just want to relax and do absolutely nothing. Do you ever have those I want to be a couch potato days? I know I do quite often. To put this in proper perspective, I'm not against rest. Rest is an essential thing that we all need to make sure we are rejuvenated and functioning properly.

Having balance in your life will give you longevity. I have learned over the years that it is healthy to take vacations, break away at times, and come back with a fresh attitude toward whatever it is you are engaged in. However, some of us are always on break, always finding a way to rest and not consistently do what needs to be done. I asked a friend that was complaining about being tired from just a short walk if he works out often. With a confident reply, he said to me, "Yes I work out and this walk shouldn't tire me out, maybe I've just had a long day." Then I asked when was the last time he actually went to the gym. "I just went to the gym a couple of weeks ago," he replied. So my next comment was, "Okay, so you work out maybe once or twice every couple of weeks or so?" As he shook his head confirming that, still not really being able to identify the problem with his answer, I knew why he was about to pass out from walking just a couple of blocks. His lack of working out on a consistent basis was starting to tell on him.

How many people know that minimal results will come from doing something one time every now and then? This is a great example of never quite breaking through to get to the level desired simply because we stop just before the real results come. How close have you been to the level you have been working on when all of a sudden you get tired and take your foot off the accelerator? What if you had just pressed on a little longer, then what? Most people have mastered working really hard, but only in spurts for very short periods of time. The winner's way is changing your mind-set to work consistently, producing steady results all the time. Author John C. Maxwell said it best: "Small disciplines repeated with consistency every day lead to great achievements gained slowly over time."

How many people can say they are great at starting a thing, but rarely ever finish? How many projects have you started working on but didn't follow through to the end? How long has this been going on? The lesson in this is when you stop and start and then stop and start all over again, you are really doing nothing but repeating the beginning step over and over. I know this because I was once an expert in starting but not finishing. That simply leaves you always at the beginning because without sticking in there long enough to complete the process, it is impossible to move forward. Any bright-eyed genius can blurt out a halfway decent idea at three in the morning, but it takes real work and consistency to actually see that idea turn into a reality.

Let's go back to my favorite example which is the gym, something I have struggled with so I feel qualified to speak on. Hypothetically, let's say a person goes to the gym this week for two days and makes it through a decent one hour workout. If this was their first time in the gym in a while then those two days were probably a struggle. The solution, however, is to keep at it so your body gets acclimated to that level of physical activity. It's sad to say, but most of us are going to take a two week break from the gym after that because our bodies are sore and it seemed much easier in theory versus actually doing it. What we don't realize is when you do go back, your body is back at square one on the struggle meter. If a person follows that routine of working out and then taking a two week break for a couple of months, they will get no results and in turn feel like something is wrong. If only you knew how many times I have said, "This gym thing doesn't work." The reality is it's not the gym - it was always my level of inconsistency at the gym that determined my results. So maybe, just maybe, it is not what you are doing toward your goals, but the level of consistency in which you are performing those actions.

I can recall having great business ideas for years, but never really doing anything to make them happen. I would even go through the act of sitting down, writing a bunch of ideas on a piece of paper, and sort of developing a plan, then not looking at that piece of paper again for weeks or even months. Eventually that piece of paper with the major business ideas on it would go missing and when my mood was right I would start yet another list of good ideas. This is called a lack of consistency. I simply had no follow through or commitment to doing anything consistently. This is the very reason why people that become great never stop practicing or perfecting whatever it is that they do. They have learned that if you don't keep the knife sharp, it will go dull. Think of anyone you admire for what they do in any area of expertise, and I am willing to bet that is a person that is constantly and consistently absorbed in what they do. They are forever studying, forever learning about their passion to such a point that they become an expert in it. Whatever your goal is, allow it to consume you so intensely that you live it and breathe it every single moment of each day.

Consistency on any level can only be accomplished if one understands what may hinder you from achieving your goals. There are enemies to consistency, and the first one is known as emotion. Your emotions can be an enemy to getting anything done in your life. Why is that? The reason is because if you base practicing off of emotions, you will only do the things necessary when you feel like it, or when you are in the right mood for it. Since your emotions or feelings may not be in the mood to do what is necessary all the time, this could be a problem.

THE THOUGHT PROCESS:

How did this consistency topic touch you?

Chapter 13

Riding the Emotional Rollercoaster

"I don't want to be at the mercy of my emotions. I want to use them, to enjoy them, and to dominate them."

~ Oscar Wilde

While most rollercoasters can be extremely exciting and some of you thrill seekers enjoy that sort of thing, this particular rollercoaster is one to avoid. The emotional rollercoaster can be an extreme enemy in your world of progress. As previously stated, achieving success in any area is a process, which means there will be some high moments as well as some low moments. The key to this is to watch how you emotionally handle each situation. Personally, I got a first class ticket to ride the emotional rollercoaster quite some time ago. It's the type of experience that you never, ever forget. At that time, I didn't know what the emotional rollercoaster was, but learned very quickly that it truly is a bumpy ride.

Fueled off of pure excitement and a zeal for life, I recall planning a network marketing event, which I bragged would bring in record numbers to anyone who would listen. I went on and on about how I would have more people at my event than anyone else who had any prior events. Back then, boasting and making lots of noise was how I hid my fear and pumped myself up a bit. Planning the event didn't seem like a hard task, and I had a solid model to follow so there were no worries there. However, it proved to not be as simple as I had originally intended. But what business or event ever is?

I began by promoting the event to family and friends. In my mind this was a piece of cake because I have a ton of family members and also some really good friends that I just knew would support me. My emotions were at an all-time high because it was sure to be the best turnout ever; after all, we all believe that the people who know and love us will always support our business endeavors, right? I pause here for a short laugh, and if you have experienced the lack of support from those you are closest to, feel free to let out a chuckle at this time also.

The day of the event came and everything was planned out. It was scheduled to start at around 7:30 p.m. and at about 7:29 p.m. when no one had arrived yet, my emotions kicked in. My first ride on the emotional rollercoaster was starting and truly taking me for a loop. Another thirty minutes passed by and still no one was there but my mother. Yeah, you know it's bad when only your mom shows up. This is the one person that will show up just because she doesn't want to hurt your feelings.

I really couldn't believe this was happening. No phone calls, no one saying I'm stuck in traffic but on the way. This was absolutely horrible to say the least. The fact that the people I thought would support me had instead bailed and didn't even have the decency to at least call to say they couldn't make it almost angered me to tears. As I write this, I'm taking a deep breath, because that is still an emotional story for me. Even right now, I can feel the anger and the sadness I felt back then. To be quite honest, my feelings were hurt that day because nothing about the outcome made any sense.

My confidence was extremely low at the time and because I didn't know about the emotional rollercoaster, I made a bad decision as a result. Emotional decisions made in the moment without any logic usually ends in terrible outcomes. My decision was that this business doesn't work and obviously it's not for me. My mother of course told me not to worry and that everything would be okay, but that didn't help because that is what mothers are supposed to say. As I was shutting everything down feeling like a complete failure, the phone rang. I answered and it was a good friend of mine named Gerald that I had invited to the event. Gerald explained that he had an emergency come up and was very sorry that he couldn't make it, but was excited to find out what I was doing. He went on to ask if we could set up another time where I could explain to him the business and exactly what the opportunity had to offer. Well you guessed right, I'm back on the emotional rollercoaster now because that one phone call took me from an extreme low to a mid-level high. In my mind, it was confirmation that maybe this thing will work out for me after all. Now please don't forget, not even five minutes before that call I had literally thrown in the towel and quit. That is just an example of how emotions can rule when you are traveling on the path to greatness. More importantly, it's an example of the irrational decisions you can make when your emotions are in total control.

The answer to riding this rollercoaster is learning how to balance your emotions and stay on an even keel no matter what is taking place. The mind-set to have in order to keep your emotions balanced is that no matter what is going on, this is just another moment that will pass. Even if it is the greatest moment ever getting excited is fine, celebrating is great, but don't allow that level of emotion to hinder what needs to be done next. The point is, please be aware of your emotions and govern them so they don't control your decision making. Allow yourself time to think and analyze your next move to decide if it is based on logic and what will promote you forward, or is it based on how you feel at that moment.

The reason how you feel at that moment is dangerous is because feelings change from moment to moment, but a decision made in that instant could last a lifetime. Be aware so that an extremely negative moment or even an extremely happy moment doesn't push you into a space where you lack consistency. The level of consistency will never be where it needs to be for success if all your decisions are based on the emotions you are feeling at the time. So pay attention because each time you make a decision the question should be: am I making the best decision that will promote progress and consistency? Literally create a habit of asking yourself this question all the time.

Some people start out in their endeavors with a burst of success. For some odd reason right off it seems like everything is going right. Each plan is working just like they thought and sometimes even exceeding expectations. So, what's wrong with that? I'm so glad you asked! The problem is, that person with the initial burst of success still has to be aware of the emotional rollercoaster. The level of excitement and joy can reach such a peak that the work it took to get there starts to taper off. Emotions can truly affect consistency in so many ways. Think about it for a second - have you ever done anything that seemed to be extremely easy for you and you gained success from it? Then all of a sudden because you are emotionally high and confident you take the success for granted and start to slack on the things needed to maintain it. Maybe you don't slack a whole lot, but the consistency level is definitely not the same as when you first started. In order to maintain that level of success, the same level of hunger you had on day one must continue to be there. The initial burst of success without guarding against the emotional rollercoaster will give a false sense of security that it is okay to take your foot off the accelerator.

Think of your favorite music artist that maybe you haven't heard any new material from in years. Now, this is just an example because obviously there can be other factors that will limit your future success. However, most of the time an artist comes out with their debut project and it skyrockets all the way to the top of the charts. Imagine having a vision for something and then all of a sudden . . . BOOM! It happens, and not only does it happen but it is even bigger than you ever imagined. Almost in an instant your life has changed because nothing is quite the same when lots of money is involved or fame comes into your life. People are suddenly nicer to you, doors open that never opened before, and access to things others may not even know exist become a part of your daily routine. In that scenario, it would be pretty easy to have an emotional moment.

What are some of the emotions that may take over at that point? Some that come to mind are; arrogance, cockiness, possessiveness, and a host of other dangerous emotions that will bankrupt your life if not managed properly. Once this begins to happen, the very things that got a person to that point don't seem as important anymore. Before the money and success an artist would spend all their time writing, staying in the studio working, or just focusing on their craft. Now, it's more about going out, pleasing the crowd, and letting this new life and its accompanying emotions overcome them. That will last for a while until it is time to reproduce that success again. That is when times become tough because the lack of staying consistent will now reveal itself when your craft is slightly off. It is exposed when material that would normally be there had you stuck to your routine is not there anymore. Then there you have it, just like the wind blows, that artist is no more. People start to ask, what happened to this person or that person? Chances are their emotions and the lack of control of those emotions pushed them off the path.

This small detail that must be incorporated in your personal development can enhance your life or if not taken seriously, can just as easily destroy it. When working to be great and accomplishing for the long-term, the aim has to be to remain consistent. When shooting a gun, if your sights are set for the middle of the target and you're hitting your target, what happens if you move even slightly to the left or the right? You got it, you miss the target altogether. So, the reason for lack of constant, consistent success most of the time in life is a failure to continue on the path without breaking stride. The reason we typically break stride is because something has affected our emotions.

How many times have you ventured off your path just because in the moment you feel a certain way? Think about that for a minute. How many times have your emotions pushed you to a point of action that didn't yield the type of results you really wanted? "Success is neither magical nor mysterious. Success is the natural consequence of consistently applying basic fundamentals." Entrepreneur Jim Rohn could not have uttered more true words than that. I love that quote. Oftentimes we get caught up looking for deeper principles or more mysterious secrets, when all along it's the foundational fundamentals, if applied on a more regular basis, which will propel us to real success. Pay attention to how you handle situations in life and ask yourself, was that reaction based on pure emotion? This takes practice because typically we don't even realize that our emotions are guiding our lives. Please don't neglect this area. It is so vital to winning over the things that life will present on your path.

THE THOUGHT PROCESS:

Have you ever taken a ride on the emotional roll-ercoaster?

Chapter 14

Success Is a Part of a System

"Imagination is everything. It is the preview of life's coming attractions."

~ Albert Einstein

Success is a part of a system that is deliberately constructed and created in one's mind. Everything about the life you desire is directly related to the life you have planned out in your mind. Further, the success you want to achieve is directly attached to your belief system. We have established that in a previous chapter, but let's examine it from a different perspective.

It's common to wish for things to happen to/for us, but it's often rare to take the time to imagine those things playing out in detail in our minds. The imagination is an amazing tool that will guide you directly to the things you desire most.

So, how would an individual create a system for success out of the things imagined? Right now if you are honest with yourself, you can recall some of the things over the course of your life that you have imagined and spent time creating in your mind. Are you thinking? Now, some of these things were not done on purpose or consciously, but because your imagination stayed focused on them they came into being. Whether those things are good or bad, truly examine the fact that somehow your mind and your imagination came up with a plan to get you to the thing or things you were focused on.

For years my mind was focused on the lack of finances in my life. I was absolutely consumed with the fact that I didn't have the money to do the things I loved or enjoyed. I would look at my bills and debt over and over again, feeling an overwhelming sense of hopelessness and doom. My imagination was so focused on it until eventually; I hit bottom and found myself surrounded by nothing but lack. My imagination and thoughts somehow allowed me to gravitate more and more to the thing that I gave the most attention to.

What do you give most of your attention to? Is your attention geared toward the problem or the solution to that problem? Is the majority of your attention focused on what you want, or what you don't want? Do you spend more time focused on what is currently there or what you plan to have soon? What is consuming you? How consumed are you by your goal or the success you want? Is it in your conversation? Do you post pictures or things to remind you of it constantly? Are you waiting for it to just happen, or are you a fanatic about making it happen?

When a person truly becomes passionate, they begin to prepare for that success right now. If you are passionate and extremely devoted to your dreams, you begin to live life as if that in which you desire has already manifested. Your level of confidence, attitude, and posture will all change at that moment.

After learning this information, I set a goal to become a millionaire. I have always had this strong zeal about no longer making money an issue in my life. To some that may sound extreme, but it is the direct opposite of the financial situation I was accustomed to. I figured if I was going to imagine and believe, might as well believe for the best. I grew up watching my mom scrape pennies together and hearing things like we just need to make ends meet. I also grew up hearing money doesn't grow on trees. Anyone ever heard that statement before? Also by the time I was twenty years old, both of my parents were deceased and I found myself fighting just to have the bare necessities. A life of just barely surviving from day-to-day was something I was no longer willing to accept. The paycheck to paycheck lifestyle was one I wanted a divorce from, and I was determined to make it happen.

I once heard that whatever consumes your mind will eventually either become or control your life. So I consumed myself with the thought of being a millionaire to such a degree that certain things just became second nature to me. Even though I wasn't a millionaire just yet, I wouldn't allow myself to say things like I can't afford this or I can't have that because of what it cost. I lived in a millionaire state of mind and consciousness from the day I decided that was what I wanted.

The system here is more mental than it is physical. The physical materialization is just an outward effect or result of an inward way of thinking, believing, and eventually knowing. The inward way of thinking and believing has to be real though, because there is no way to trick the belief system to bringing something into being you only partially believe. The physical life is a product of the mental life. Again, it goes back to everything being created in the mind. The mind is the battlefield, and the fight is either won or lost there. Artist Jameson Frank said: "Our greatest battles are that with our own minds." If you show me a person with a strong belief system in what they desire to the point where they don't accept anything less than their thoughts, I will show you someone with a quality of life that is equivalent to what they think about. Once you figure out how powerful the mind is and that you are able to create any situation, life truly changes.

To construct the life you envision requires changing the thoughts that limit you. And in order to change the thoughts that limit you, one must examine every part of the life you live currently. The point is to see how many contradictions there are in your current life versus the life you want to create.

Have you ever considered that the limitations are all mental? Perhaps you believe that because of where you come from or the fact that no one else you know personally has reached the level you aspire to be at, that it is impossible for you as well. That was my dilemma at one point. This is usually a big obstacle to overcome. No one ever wants to admit that maybe subconsciously you think that you just aren't good enough to achieve your dream or accomplish something huge. Also subconsciously, we often believe that the goal is so enormous that it is simply unattainable. This is not an easy thing to admit because it's easier to trick yourself into thinking this is not the case.

I can tell you firsthand that I discovered this was a huge challenge for me and many other people I have encountered. Now on the surface I was confident, and no one from the outside looking in would ever know that deep down I had a serious fear of failing. Failure was something I had been exposed to so much that in the back of my mind a fear had been created, and it was holding me back. There was something about the struggles I had seen growing up and the struggles I experienced as an adult which made me subconsciously think that getting beyond that was impossible. Once I was able to admit that to myself, I decided to attack the fear that my success wouldn't happen. In order to do that, I had to change my belief system or reprogram myself. It took some time to reconstruct my thinking to such a point where consciously and subconsciously I was not able to see, comprehend, talk about, or even entertain anything but that which had permeated every fiber of my being.

Trust me on this; people will think you are strange. It is hard for others to comprehend you when the outside life you live has not yet caught up with the inner life that you have created. There is a period of time that will go by before the inner and the outer lives meet up and connect. The time period before the inner and outer you meet up and materialize is what's known as the process. During the process you have to remember to feed the imagination with everything that goes in line with what you want to create.

Also it's imperative to starve the imagination from taking in anything that is not aligned or even slightly contrary to what you are working to produce in your life.

To live a life where your inward desires and goals become the only thing you willingly accept may seem crazy to some, but if your mind locks in on that then indeed you are preparing yourself to live that way outwardly. The complex part is not quitting just before the outward catches up with what is going on inwardly. The reason that part is so complex is because no one can really tell you how long your process will last. This is the part where individuality plays a major role because the process is preparing you to handle whatever materialization will be produced. No one knows exactly how much prep time you need to be ready for that manifestation. Either the time frame of the process will stop the majority of people, or they allow some outward limitation, such as a relative, a friend, or some circumstance to reverse the inward creation that has been established. Additionally, telling any and everyone your vision is not always the best idea because even the people you love the most may not be able to see what you inwardly see. If you listen to them, they could give you their version of a reality check that takes you completely off the path. The reality is, winners create their own truth and are not subject to the reality that society or other people have set.

The rapper, actor, and activist Tupac Shakur made this statement: "Reality is wrong. Dreams are for real." That is one of the main points of what this entire book is about. The mental strategies in this book are meant to assist you in creating whatever your mind can dream and imagine. To win and not just survive is to step outside of the usual, defy the odds, and create the unexpected. The key to life is being bold about what you want; you can't be afraid of what you see with your physical eyes. As long as your vision or your mind can see beyond that, then you know all is well. The only time to worry is when your mind cannot see beyond the physical circumstances. I will say it again: you don't see with your eyes, you see through them. The moment a person learns to see with their mind and their mind has been reprogrammed to see exactly what they desire, your entire world changes for the better.

This system of success is not about the mechanics of what it takes to write a business plan, or what tax status you should list your company under. All that stuff has its place, but the system of success is mainly about you. You are the common denominator in any business, career, goal, or whatever your aspiration might be. It's about designing everything about you as a person to reflect the very thing you want.

What things in your life today currently reflect what you desire? What things in your life today don't reflect what you desire? One huge factor I always look at when someone tells me they are working on going to a new level is how they speak and act. The way you speak and carry yourself will let me know right away if you truly believe what you want is possible and can see it in your mind.

One of my goals has always been to own a business that has an international presence. Now, some people may say that is a really big goal considering the fact that most small businesses today never even get clients outside of their own city. Well my first task was to make sure that I never listened to statistics on what most businesses do. In my mind, I never planned to be like most businesses in the first place, so what those businesses do have absolutely nothing to do with me. Can you feel my attitude? Can you feel my level of confidence? I didn't know it at the time but I was building that system of success in my mind even back then. The more I took myself out of the categories that society or the people around me tried to put me in, the more I could see my business being an international company.

However, it didn't just stop with my way of thinking; my attitude and level of confidence in what I had built transferred over into the way I spoke about my business and also the way I acted when it came to business. From day one of creating the concept for my business, it was always regarded as a multimillion dollar international life changing company. In addition, my company and my brand were always considered a household name in my eyes. I never called my business just a small start-up business, nor did I ever think or refer to it as just something local.

I absolutely hate when people tell me they have a "side business" – what exactly does that mean? Please understand that I do relate to the concept of "side business" because society and all of its corrupt programming has taught us that if you work a job for someone else and have a little ambition outside of that job, then that is something you do on the side. My question is, did you create the thing outside of that job to always be something you just do as a hobby? If so, then disregard what I am about to say next.

For those of you that created the thing "on the side" to free you from some nine-to-five corporate job that you have no passion for, then I dare you to speak of that business as if it is the only thing you do. I absolutely dare you to treat that business with more respect and importance than you do the job that you go to just to get a paycheck. If you do, your "side business" will soon be the only business you will have to pay attention to. I lived this existence day in and day out until the business I created while working at someone else's job became not only something I did full-time, but it also developed into an international business right before my very eyes. My system of thinking opened up doors that no one could close. I demanded that the universe give me exactly what I wanted for one reason and one reason only – because I refused to take no for answer.

What do you anticipate to receive, and why do you keep accepting no for an answer? When what you want becomes who and what you are, then there is no way it can't happen for you.

People that achieve things that seem to be outside of the norm in this world consume themselves in what they do. They mentally transform into the goal or accomplishment, therefore becoming all they want to be. They become purpose driven and each day is yet another exciting journey to explore their goal on a deeper level. So you want to be an NBA player one day, but you never study film of the great players and you only play the game maybe once a week if you feel like it. Now, seriously ask yourself, does that reflect a future NBA Hall of Fame member? You are your greatest asset, or you can be your greatest liability.

How do you make sure that the things you do and see are conducive for exactly what you want to create? The goal is to create the life you want inside of you even before the life you want outside of you is present.

Here is the question to ask yourself daily: Did anything I do today push me closer toward my goal? Did my thoughts today reflect more on what I want, or more on what I don't want? This is where honesty really comes into play, because lying to yourself is a definite tragedy. If you can answer that question with an honest "no", then it is time to change some things.

No matter what you are reaching for in life the time is now to go after it, and every day you allow time to go by without doing something that gets you one step closer to that goal is just wasting time. Even if you have to say what you desire to yourself over and over again throughout the day until you start to believe it, do that. I actually recommend that.

There are no rules here and no time to worry about how outrageous a principle may seem. This is about getting results, and if talking to yourself will convince you and train your belief system to produce results, then do it. Think about the simple things that can be done to assist you on a daily basis in becoming all you desire to be. Even if that thing is just research on whatever you want, that is a better start than doing nothing at all. What does your system consist of? If you don't have systematic operations you do daily to build the life you expect to see, then is it realistic to think that those things you want will happen with absolutely no help from you?

THE THOUGHT PROCESS:

Does your mind typically focus on the problem, or the solution to that problem?

Chapter 15

Waiting Can Be Costly

"My mother always told me I wouldn't amount to anything because I procrastinate. I said, 'Just wait.'"

~ Judy Tenuta

It's raining outside and I can hear the huge drops hitting the pavement from my bedroom window. This is one of those mornings that makes me just want to get back in bed and throw the covers over my head. However, a new day has begun and that means there is work to be done.

From the moment my eyes open, there is a ping here and a ring there. Those are the sounds from my cell phone alerting me to several calls, text messages, e-mails, IM messages, etc. I'm sure many of you can relate and understand exactly what I mean. Those are the typical noises that alert me to the fact that the day has begun. I usually take a minute, meditate, and just imagine how great I expect the day to go. After that, business and all the details that go along with the day are yelling for my attention. All the tasks that must be accomplished that day remind me of that old Dunkin' Donuts commercial where the guy says: "It's time to make the donuts!" That just means it's time to work. My brain then refers to the saying, "Only the strong will survive."

I'm laughing because that is the way it seems at times. Almost like a boxer in the ring about to go twelve rounds with life and when your eyes open, it's like the bell has rung. At that point you either step up or get knocked out. It is so easy to just turn it all off and wait until another time to deal with the responsibilities and things life will present for the day. However, I have programmed myself to know that waiting is costly and procrastination kills dreams. The writer Charles Dickens said: "Procrastination is the thief of time, collar him." So I make it my business to arrest procrastination and throw it out of my life as often as possible.

With that being said, I shower and get dressed. While showering, as the water rushes over my head I say to myself, "No matter what happens today, I will be victorious and favored in every situation. Things will go well for me on this day." Just like that, my winning attitude is set and I am off to conquer the world.

How do you start your day? How do you set your mind and attitude to achieve for that day? How do you fight procrastination and the temptation to just wait and put things off until another time?

Time is always of the essence. Time is the one thing that no one has figured out how to get more of in a single day. No matter who you are or how special you might be, we all get the same twenty-four hours in a day. Now in theory, that sounds like a lot of time, right? It would seem like one could do everything they wanted to within a twenty-four hour time frame, so why is time always an issue? Why is time the thing most people complain about? Let's take a moment to carefully examine these twenty-four hours a little bit further. I want to first subtract some of that time for things we all must do. These are the mandatory things in life that will typically subtract productivity time from your day.

The number one thing is sleep; the body must rest at some point. No matter who you are and how hard you push yourself, at some point the body will sleep with or without your permission. Let's just say you are not average and only need about seven hours of sleep, then those twenty-four hours are now down to seventeen hours. Time is already starting to dwindle.

Another mandatory thing that can take up time in the day is nourishing the body. I will push the envelope here and say most of you eat three times a day, and I know some of you may not but let's just say that is average. Now, some of you may have found a way to eat quickly and still be productive at the same time. I applaud your effort on that because sometimes it is a must. However, for the sake of people that don't prefer to eat quickly, I will say an additional three hours minimum is spent eating. Well you are now down to fourteen hours left in your day. If by any chance you are an individual that works a traditional nine-to-five job to make a living, then a whole lot of the rest of the day will be taken up also. Just for the sake of example let's also subtract an eight hour workday from the fourteen hours that are left. By doing that a person is only left with about six hours in a day. Now assuming you don't squander that time watching television, texting a friend, or updating your social media pages, six hours is not bad and it's enough time to be productive. However, isn't it easy for those final six hours to just pass by without you even knowing where the time went?

Oh and I forgot to mention people that have kids and other mandatory responsibilities, that alone may take up the rest of the day. I said all of that to say, no one has any time to wait or to waste for that matter. Time is such a valuable resource because it is simply irreplaceable. Once a moment passes, it's gone and there is no way to ever get that same moment back. Some people have even debated with me, declaring, "Well, if a person doesn't get whatever they need done in these twenty-four hours then they have another twenty-four hours to work with the next day." Do they really? Are you sure about that? The fact of the matter is, when you close your eyes at night there is no guarantee that you will wake up tomorrow to experience another twenty-four. This literally means, every time we wait to do something we want to do, something we have planned to do, or just something we enjoy doing, we risk not having another opportunity to make it happen. The artist Pablo Picasso put it this way, "Only put off until tomorrow what you are willing to die having left undone."

So, the moral of this story is maximizing all the time you have right now. Please don't be deceived to believe that "later" exists. The goal here is to get you to view time in such a way that every second becomes valuable to you. If someone told you that you only had two days to live, how would you spend your time? If within those forty-eight hours you had to accomplish as many goals as possible and leave your mark on the world, how would you work? Would you wait? Would you put something off just because you weren't in the mood to do it right then? Remember I said earlier there is no guarantee there will be a later, so take advantage of the power of NOW. The principle here is never leaving a stone unturned. If there is something that needs to be done get it done right then and there. Putting it off will only make it more difficult to do.

Over the years I have discovered this thing in life called grace. The term grace as I want to define it is a level of favor as in a divine presence that opens a door in order for things to work out for your benefit. The key here is that favor door will not stay open forever. When grace is upon you, there is no time to wait; it is all about action.

What do I mean? Over the years I have been the king of waiting and putting things off until later. I was notorious for getting an idea and saying okay I will definitely do that later, but I would notice that later the idea didn't have the same level of excitement attached to it, and seemed very difficult to implement. When I would finally get around to doing the thing that sort of came to me out of nowhere, it would seem as if I had missed the opportunity to take advantage of it. It was either that or later I would totally forget the exact details that originally made the idea special or unique. Has anyone ever experienced that before? In a sense, it was almost like I missed out on the perfect timing to implement the thought or idea that had come to mind.

I remember attending church one Sunday, and during what seemed to be an otherwise routine sermon the pastor interjected one unforgettable sound bite, "Don't miss out on the grace period." To be honest, I didn't pay it much attention until later when it hit me that everything has a grace period attached to it and once the grace period is up, it becomes difficult to take full advantage of the benefits that were only provided for that window of time. In complete and total shock, in that moment I got what is known as a revelation or revealed knowledge and for once I knew exactly how I had missed a lot of opportunities to excel over the years.

Last year one day before my birthday, I decided to get out and enjoy the sunshine. My plan was to take a drive with the sunroof open. Now in Atlanta where I live during the summer when the sun is out, that means it's extremely hot (they don't call it Hotlanta for nothing!). My goal was to get my car washed so the sun could beam off my clean car and I could take a drive knowing that my car was looking good. Ever had that I want a super clean car moment? Ever wanted to just lean and profile in your clean car as you ride down the street? Maybe that was just how I was feeling that day.

Anyway, when it's super-hot that also means that it could rain at any moment. In fact, it can storm and the sun will remain shining bright the entire time. So I went to a car wash and as soon as they finished detailing my car it started to rain. The guy at the car wash, I think his name was Joe or James. Let's call him James for today – told me that as long as I brought the car back within three business days I could get it washed again for free since it was raining. Now follow me on this: James gave me a receipt and it stated clearly that I could get a free wash as long as I came back in no later than three business days from that date. That receipt and what it guaranteed me was my grace period. It's pretty simple, all I had to do was show up, present my receipt, and get a free wash. There would be no questions asked or problems because of the grace period I had to do so. Well, let me tell you what happened and how I learned that grace is so important. The person that I was then and the mind-set I had put off going back to the car wash because I kept telling myself I could do it later.

About four days passed and I noticed that my car was dirty as ever so I returned and tried to claim my free wash. When I got back to the car wash, James was there and I presented him with my receipt for the free wash. He looked at me and in a very kind voice said, "Sir, your receipt has expired for the free wash." He stated that they would be more than happy to wash my car at the regular price. I was a bit upset and tried to reason with him that it had only been an extra day since the receipt had expired. Then all of a sudden it hit me, my grace period of favor at the car wash was over. Due to the grace period being over, it was a whole lot more difficult to get what I wanted done (for free, anyway). In essence I had missed my window of favor or my window of opportunity.

The point is, this is what happens to us when it comes to our goals and the things we want to do in life. We get a thought, a great business idea, or something we want to do and instead of doing it right then when that grace period and favor is there, we wait. By the time we get around to doing it, our receipt has expired and we wonder why it's so difficult to make things happen at that point. That idea to call a certain person came to mind but instead of doing it, you figured it would be okay to just call them later. However, when you try to reach them later all you get is voice mail for the next week or so. The reason for that is the window of opportunity is now closed. This doesn't mean that your goal can't happen; it just means it will be more difficult than it has to be. Why take the difficult route when you can take the favored route? Why not just do it right then while the window of grace is open? It will definitely make your life a whole lot easier. I had to learn this lesson the hard way, and I think back to how many things in my life didn't work out the way I wanted or needed them to because I waited until my grace period had expired. Now I say it time and time again, waiting can be very costly.

When it comes to pursuing your goals this is the best advice I have ever received: The best time to pursue a dream is right now. The exact moment when you know what you want is the time to go after it. People want to wait until their money is in order, or the kids are in college, or when they make enough money on their job to walk away and start doing what they love. How many of you know those things rarely happen in that way? The perfect scenario to do something will rarely come about. Life has to be approached with a mentality like there is no tomorrow and since I only have today I will do all I can and not wait for something to come down the line.

I remember my first "real" job – the kind where you get benefits and all that stuff. I was working at a local bank sorting mail into these tiny little slots all day. The job paid a low wage, and every day I would come home with the most severe paper cuts you can ever imagine. I knew I had to do something different because I did not want to continue at this job for the rest of my life. So I took action and began to learn how to be an entrepreneur and work for myself. If I had waited, I may still be sorting mail at that bank today. Nothing about my situation at that time said it would be smart to try to be an entrepreneur. I pause because I know how close I was to not pursuing my goal of being a business owner and saying I would do it another time or at a later date. To think, I almost never became a business owner in the first place because honestly I had no money.

Now when most people say they have no money they still have savings or something put aside and just prefer not to use that money. That was definitely not the case for me; I really had no money at all. I was a young kid in my late teens with a low paying job and a heart full of hope and ambition. My dad was deceased and my mother was battling a very serious illness, so there was no one I could even borrow money from. An incredible opportunity came my way that would put me in business for myself along with the necessary help it would take for me to truly have success at such a young age. I was all in with both feet until this gentleman by the name of Mr. Bigbee whispered in my ear the up-front investment it would cost to take advantage of this opportunity. Can someone say nothing in life is free? At the time I didn't understand that and pretty much wrote the opportunity off because there was no way I could come up with that type of money in my current position. My mind-set was I would just keep working hard and one day I would have the money to invest in something of this nature.

Have you ever said I will do this or that one day when I have the extra money? That "one day" mentality is a surefire way to kill your dreams. That "one day" where you will just all of a sudden have a huge lump sum of money to do all you desire won't just materialize out of thin air. That is the "do it later" mentality, the assumption that tomorrow is promised and something miraculous will just happen.

The gentleman Mr. Bigbee, who would later become a mentor and a big brother to me, asked me a very serious question that day. That particular question forever changed my life and that is where this mentality of never waiting and aggressively going after what you want was born. Mr. Bigbee asked, "If you continue doing what you've been doing for the next year, do you think you will have the investment money then?" Now honestly that question was like getting stung by a bee, it was quick but it hurt like hell. Mr. Bigbee was a young well-dressed guy that looked like he had all the money in the world; but in that current state of mind I wanted to punch him in the face. It felt like he was trying to insult me, but I had to humble myself and truly consider what he was asking. I had to be honest with myself and say that if I continue to do what I've been doing, I'm only going to get the same results that I've been getting. To do the same thing over and over again expecting a different result is classified as insane. At that moment, the light bulb went off and I said no matter what, I will make a way.

I made a decision to take an aggressive approach to making my life what I knew I desired and deserved. I gave Mr. Bigbee my word, and literally three days later I had the necessary monies to get involved in that business venture. With that push and level of determination, I became a business owner at the age of eighteen years old. I definitely won't say it was easy to make it happen but it was necessary. I think back to that day and wonder what if I would have waited and not made it happen right then? Where would I be today? That first business venture set the stage and taught me everything needed for the future businesses I would start. I could very well still be in a terrible position today had I not made a strategic move.

So what is it that you are waiting to do? What perfect day or scenario are you waiting on before you act on your goals? Here is a clue in case this chapter didn't spell it out clearly enough - that perfect day to execute may never come. While we wait on the perfect day and just the right climate, think of how much time we are wasting in the process.

Now, please remember the corresponding action principle here. In that time, I didn't do anything so extreme that it would be detrimental to me. I did however make some serious sacrifices and maybe missed a bill payment or two in order to get that investment money. However, for me I knew how much my investment would yield and the time frame in which I would get a return. So even though I sacrificed, I was still a master at strategizing my move so that it was well thought out and not just an impulse move with no plan attached to it. Everything in this book as far as practicing before the game is concerned works together, and it's critical that you think and consider all that you have learned. Those thoughts that come while reading are so vital because those are specific strategies for what fits your life and situation.

Again the goal is to challenge you to think through your own situations. The points in this book are the guidelines which you can use as you plot your next move. Wisdom is achieved when one practices things that have been well thought out and willingly modify them along the way to perfection. Wisdom is gained as one takes steps toward the things they desire. The one thing for sure is that wisdom is not operating as long as we just wait and hope some miracle happens. Once you are on this path of thinking to win, strategizing before making a move, considering all possible outcomes, and preparing ahead of time, insight into all situations will become second nature. When things come up, you will begin to see all angles and learn to decipher which direction or move is the best for you in that moment.

Notice the statement says thinking to win, not thinking to survive. There is a huge difference between the two. If I was only thinking to survive back then I may have waited and saved money little by little until eventually the investment money was there. The only problem with that would have been there would be no guarantee that the opportunity would still be there. So, the winner mentality figures out the best possible way to win, operates during the grace period, but still does things in the most intelligent and strategic way.

THE THOUGHT PROCESS:

What are you waiting on?

SECTION VI: WINNERS ARE NEVER ORDINARY

"Opinions of the masses kill the 'extra' in an extraordinary idea."

~ Mokokoma Mokhonoana

There is something very distinct about you. The way you think, the way you perceive things, and even the way you express your beliefs. There is something about you that doesn't seem quite normal, and I use that word in the sense of not being just like everyone else. Even though there were times that you played the role and did the best acting job possible to fit in, that never quite worked. Overall, your thought process just didn't fully correspond with everyone else. In other words for some reason you have always had thoughts and ideas that were considered outside the box. All your life you have seen things in a bigger way or in a different way from most people you talk to. Maybe you have never truly been able to explain what that X factor is. The smallest thing to someone else will be something grand to you, and vice versa. Someone else may want to play for the team, but your thought might have been how can I own the team?

As a kid all your friends wanted to go to the corner store to buy candy, but you were the one that decided to buy it in bulk at a lower price and sell it to them for a profit. What is that about? Why did you go left when typically you were supposed to go right? For some reason when it was time to zig, you zagged. No matter what situation occurs in life, even the worst case scenario, to you there is always a way out. That way out may seem like a long journey but there is no such thing as defeat in your mind; it must work out.

That doesn't mean you don't get frustrated or have challenging moments, but somehow you always bounce back. No matter how low you have been, for some reason you still had an element of hope. The level of optimism that you possess is beyond what most can fathom to the degree that others may think you are strange. Trust me, I understand completely. I live in a world where my level of optimism has made me an outcast at times. For example, have you ever said something to a group of people and everyone looked at you funny? They looked at you that way because whatever you said was so far outside of their realm of thinking that they couldn't comprehend the point that was being made.

Now, you may not classify yourself as a rebel but then again some of you may identify with that, too. Maybe your distinct attributes have placed you in the category of being a bit eccentric.

In any regard, following all the rules to the letter serves you in no way, shape, or form. I'm not talking about breaking laws or disrupting the flow of society. Then again if you are the type of person I think you are, you understood that anyway. What am I talking about? It's the way you think and believe in life that makes you peculiar. It's your creativity, or maybe even the willingness to attempt the impossible. It's the way you express yourself or how you view situations with a perspective that typically no one else would see as you do. It's your atypical nature that tends to set you apart from the crowd. The way you analyze something and see the intricate details that others are not able to see or just don't pay attention to. All your friends wanted to get good jobs and retire after forty years, but your mind always wanted to make millions by the time you were thirty, or retire at forty-five rather than sixty-seven.

There is nothing wrong with you just in case you are wondering. There is also nothing wrong with the person that plays for the team or the person that owns it. There is nothing wrong with the person that walks the straight path just like the rest of society. If that is their preference and accepted by them, then it's perfectly fine. Most of the time that person has just suppressed their X factor in order to fit in to such a degree that they can't recognize it anymore. However, for you suppressing that X factor was never an option.

I'm here to let you know that those distinctions about you are just signs of the winner status in you fighting to get out of you. Those things that other people may not understand about you will serve as the thing that sets you apart and makes you great. The truth is that we all have thought outside of the ordinary before, but some of us restrain ourselves because we feel playing it safe and coloring inside the lines is what we are supposed to do. Are you suppressing the unique attributes that make you who you are? What outside of the ordinary trait do you typically dismiss because you don't want to seem weird? What gift do you have that is unlike anyone else that you need to share with the world?

Winners are never ordinary, which simply means that no two people will walk the exact same path. When you find yourself trying to mold your path exactly like the next person knowing that it does not feel right to you, then something is probably wrong. When you are merely copying someone else, that is making yourself ordinary and dismissing the difference that will make you great. Embrace all the things about you that are different than the next person. In order to become extraordinary, it will require going outside of the ordinary and dancing to music some may not even hear playing. Winners aren't ordinary; they do what others won't do to get to places others won't get to.

Instead of trying to hide your differences or contain them, figure out how it plays a role in your strategic plan to fulfillment. That is what personal development is all about; it's the development of who you really are. To dig deep within and pull out that gift or talent that has been bestowed upon you. Then take that gift or talent and perfect it so that no one in the world does what you do quite like you.

THE THOUGHT PROCESS:

What do you consider different about you? What unique attribute(s) have you overlooked?

Chapter 16

Personal and Professional Development

"He who conquers others is strong; He who conquers himself is mighty"
~ Lao Tzu

Traveling and meeting people of all races, cultures, and ethnicities has taught me that overall people basically have the same desires. Most of the time people want to know how they can advance in their career, or how they can improve their business. People typically want to know what they can do in order to professionally excel. After all, we all want more out of life.

Everyone in some capacity is trying to improve their status to become bigger and better. The "more" complex is huge because no matter where you go, "more" is all around us. Everywhere you turn, there is an advertisement about something that is bigger and better than what you currently have. People want everything supersized – more cars, more clothes, more houses, or a better quality of all of those things. How do I make more money is typically the number one question I am asked. In no way am I opposed to this question, and I am definitely not opposed to people making more money and creating the type of lifestyle they have dreamed about. In fact I encourage people to continue to excel and grow higher in that aspect.

But I have discovered that people want a concrete answer that they can apply and magically make more money overnight. No one wants to hear about the process or steps it will take to develop a higher level of thinking that will produce overall success and unlimited income. We live in a microwave society, so people want you to give them the "secret" that will work right now. However, I finally understand that while professional development is extremely necessary to get ahead, it comes second to the fundamentals that are taught through personal development.

Often when a client specifically asks, "How do I make more money," I will refer people to certain books or principles they should adapt to their lives. Ninety-nine percent of the time, those books and principles will have to do with personal development, strategic thinking, problem solving, and/or spiritual connection, and not solely about making money or professional success.

This one gentleman named Carlos, who is a great guy and on his way to doing some incredible things, once sent me a very frustrated e-mail. He stated that there must have been a mix up because the things I referred for him to read had nothing to do with how to turn his current portfolio into millionaire status. The information was strictly about learning who he was as a person, and dealt with developing the internal structure that it takes to deal with huge success. The information that was suggested had a lot to do with character and attitude, which are two components in building a solid foundation. The eye-opener that most people never stick around to find out is, if you invest in the personal development side then the professional side will thrive that much more. The issue is personal development takes time, energy, effort, money, and a few other things that sound like too much of a hassle. The reality is, we all will personally develop either through our own conscious plan or through the hardships we fall into as a result of neglecting to create a solid foundation. I will leave that choice up to you. As author John C. Maxwell would say, "A great life starts within."

Money for example is supposed to be an asset, but if you have not developed personally then money can be a huge liability. Everyone who is on the quest to get tons of money in their lives should be careful, because it may not be exactly what you expected. Getting money is sort of like when Dorothy, the Lion, the Scarecrow, and the Tin Man finally made it to meet the Wizard of Oz. It was a hell of a journey to get there but once you arrive and pull back the curtain, you learn it wasn't exactly how everyone else made it seem. Maybe the reality doesn't end in disappointment, but some of the pros and cons involved were just never expected.

Yes, there are some areas that money will help you in, but it is not the answer to all things as some may think. Money is an amplifier, which means it will increase who and what you currently are. If you are a caring, giving, loving person that has a desire to help people, then money will amplify that and in turn you will be able to make a bigger contribution and impact. On the other hand, if you are a deceitful, evil, narcissistic, uncaring type of person, money will just make you like that even more. "Money and success don't change people; they merely amplify what is already there." Actor Will Smith made that statement and it is absolutely true. How many people would agree with that?

Personal and professional development goes together but everything starts at the personal development level. At BORN II WIN, which is my inspirational speaking and coaching company, we define personal and professional development as the internal and external components to build a winning lifestyle that is sustainable and fulfilling. Its one thing to build a winning lifestyle, but it's more important to have the foundation in place so that lifestyle is sustainable and fulfilling.

Personal development is the internal, which is the mind-set, way of thinking, and belief system. This is where the path to any level of greatness should start. On this foundation, professional success can be built on solid ground that is able to support it. There can be no professional development if the personal development is not initially in place. This goes back to practicing and preparation. It is possible to professionally reach all of the goals you have ever desired, but if that is short-lived and the only area of success in your life, how good will it be? What would be the point of achieving but not being ready to sustain it, then watch it all crumble before your eyes? Yes, you can cheat your way past the personal development and only focus on the professional, but the professional will then be incomplete. So let's start with the personal development and establish that foundation for real success. I define real success as not just a pretty picture. Fake success is when it only looks good on the outside and truly you are living in quiet desperation on the inside because it is all just a façade.

Every chapter of this book has been about how you develop personally. That is the basis of what the strategic mind is all about. The reason for that is there is a method to the madness of achieving. Personal development is put in place so that the ability to professionally achieve is possible. Sustainable success comes with a huge price and responsibility. If you pay attention to the truly successful in our society, most of them have stories of being miserable at times. Some of them even create habit forming addictions that eventually lead to their demise. Personally, I have been in the presence of some extremely successful, wealthy people that tell me they would trade it all in tomorrow for real fulfillment and happiness.

What am I saying? Just because someone is professionally successful in life does not necessarily make them happy, and it doesn't make them complete. When I hear people say they would trade it all in because they are miserable, it lets me know that the personal development side was not fully set before the professional side came into existence. The level of character, integrity, responsibility, and ability to deal with what comes when everything you ever wanted is suddenly in your possession takes time to develop.

Michael Jackson was and still is one of the greatest entertainers this world has ever known. Michael reached a level of achievement that is often imitated by many but duplicated by few, at least not on the grand scale in which he did it. This gentleman became an icon all over the world. There is not a place on earth that you can go and say his name and people of all ages don't know who he is. His legacy and music lives on today to the point that when any song that Michael ever made comes on, we all sing along unconsciously. Practically every single song he ever made was a hit, and the memories of those tunes are forever etched in our souls. No matter what race, culture, or ethnicity you are, his talent broke down all of those barriers. The success Michael created was simply universal. The level of talent, work ethic, and professional perfection that he had simply amazes me. All of the wealth, fame, and accolades that any human being could ever ask for, Michael attained.

Yet in the midst of all that, Michael often talked about times when he was depressed and unhappy. We have all read stories and seen interviews where he spoke of not feeling like a real person due to the nature of his life. According to an article in The Huffington Post entitled "'It Hurts to Be Me': Confessions of Michael Jackson," the icon once said: "People think they know me, but they really don't. Not really. Actually, I am one of the loneliest people on this earth. I cry sometimes, because it hurts. It does. To be honest, I guess you could say that it hurts to be me." Most people cannot even fathom being depressed with that much professional success going on in their lives. This is just proof that our society has given professional success and wealth more credit than it's due.

Consider the facts here: from a very young age, Michael was a famous entertainer. He was never fortunate enough to truly experience life without the public eye watching his every move. To experience life without the criticism or stress of maintaining this image the world always wanted to see. So from a kid with fortune and fame to an adult with even more fortune and fame, the guy never had the chance to truly personally develop and live. The chance to learn how to cultivate great relationships, or to see if people really liked him just for the person he was instead of what he had accomplished. The opportunity to truly get to know the man, and not the image that was created for public consumption. When I read his story and analyzed it, clearly that life was a difficult one to lead. Everything that is precious about life from a personal standpoint, he was robbed of just to give the world his talent. Now, we definitely appreciate his talent and all he gave us, but that was an unfair price for any human being to pay. Personal development involves learning how to become a balanced person so that you don't end up with a lot of professional accolades, yet miserable because all the other components that make life a joy have been neglected. Michael wasn't offered much of a choice, but we can learn from that and not create a life that is just about professional success.

Life is meant to be lived in every sense of that word. Please don't get caught up in just creating financial success as most of us do and become bankrupt in other areas. The great professional golfer Ben Hogan made a great point when he said, "As you walk down the fairway of life you must smell the roses, for you only get to play one round." Unfortunately, we don't have the option to do life over again, so be sure to build a life that is not just professionally successful but personally fulfilling.

There will never be, nor have you ever seen, a brinks truck following a hearse. That means no matter how much money you make, when life is over that money will remain here to be divided among others. So don't give money and professional success more attention than it is due.

Where is your focus when it comes to life successes? Is the focus on materials things, fancy titles, and how much wealth you can attain? Maybe the focus is on power and control because embedded in you somewhere is someone that just wants some real attention. I truly hope that right now your mind is focusing on what is important about life. This book talks about a lot of variables to consider as you plot your plan to win in life. The most important thing is not to forget to live and spend time on things that truly matter. There are several areas of success in life, and if any of these areas are neglected then you can end up very incomplete. Professional achievement and attaining wealth does have its role in success, but to think that is the only thing success is about is definitely inaccurate.

Be sure to have a balanced approach to your growth and development. Spend as much time cultivating great relationships as you do on the business plan. Spend as much time focusing on your spiritual life and well-being as you do balancing the business accounts. Also please take time to invest in your health and the proper maintenance of your physical body as you do the dream car that you plan to purchase. Please don't make the professional mechanics so important that the personal fundamentals are neglected. I really can't stress this point enough. That is the reason I keep saying it over and over again because I want to drill it in your conscious and subconscious mind.

Build your human capital before building the monetary capital, and the monetary capital will last longer. The idea is to become the person that is not always chasing success, yet constantly evolving into the person that is worthy of success always chasing you.

THE THOUGHT PROCESS:

Personal or professional development – which have you been more focused on?

Chapter 17

Never Do Just What Is Expected

"When you perform at a level that is just what is expected, you have bought a ticket to the mediocrity club's largest event"

~ Dr. Shawna Woodruff

I recall sitting and complaining with everyone else at a former job because the place seemed to really give true meaning to the term "glass ceiling." The glass ceiling is when you have reached that peak where a company will not allow you to go any higher. I remember being in the break room listening to people talk about how they had worked at this company for years and couldn't remember the last time they got a raise in pay. It was truly a pity party, and no one had any solutions to this dilemma. It just appeared as if there was no room for advancement. Every day it seemed like I was living in a world where I was stuck in a hole and there was no sign of a rope to help me climb out. Somehow I knew what seemed to be a dead end job could not be the end to my story. As I was home one weekend sitting in my favorite chair flipping channels, I heard a televangelist tell the story in the Bible about the five talents. Ever hear that one before? Well, the parable in Matthew 25:14–30 (Amplified Bible) goes like this: For it is like a man who was about to take a long journey, and he called his servants together and entrusted them with his property.15 To

one he gave five talents [probably about $5,000], to another two,
to another one—to each in proportion to his own [a]personal
ability. Then he departed and left the country.16 He who had
received the five talents went at once and traded with them, and
he gained five talents more.17 And likewise he who had received
the two talents—he also gained two talents more. 18 But he who
had received the one talent went and dug a hole in the ground
and hid his master's money. 19 Now after a long time the master
of those servants returned and settled accounts with them. 20
And he who had received the five talents came and brought him
five more, saying, Master, you entrusted to me five talents; see,
here I have gained five talents more. 21 His master said to him,
Well done, you upright (honorable, [b]admirable) and faithful
servant! You have been faithful and trustworthy over a little; I
will put you in charge of much. Enter into and share the joy (the
delight, the [c]blessedness) which your master enjoys. 22 And he
also who had the two talents came forward, saying, Master, you
entrusted two talents to me; here I have gained two talents more.
23 His master said to him, Well done, you upright (honorable,
[d]admirable) and faithful servant! You have been faithful and
trustworthy over a little; I will put you in charge of much. Enter
into and share the joy (the delight, the [e]blessedness) which
your master enjoys. 24 He who had received one talent also came
forward, saying, Master, I knew you to be a harsh and hard man,
reaping where you did not sow, and gathering where you had not
winnowed [the grain]. 25 So I was afraid, and I went and hid your
talent in the ground. Here you have what is your own. 26 But
his master answered him, You wicked and lazy and idle servant!
Did you indeed know that I reap where I have not sowed and
gather [grain] where I have not winnowed? 27 Then you should
have invested my money with the bankers, and at my coming I
would have received what was my own with interest. 28 So take
the talent away from him and give it to the one who has the ten
talents. 29 For to everyone who has WILL more be given, and he
will be [f]furnished richly so that he will have an abundance; but
from the one who does not have, even what he does have will be

taken away. 30 And throw the good–for–nothing servant into the outer darkness; there will be weeping and grinding of teeth.

Now please allow me to explain this as the televangelist did on that day. I know it sounds a bit harsh, but there is such a powerful lesson behind this story. The guy with one talent didn't do anything extra in order to increase that in which he had. In other words, he didn't even attempt to do anything above and beyond in order to get better results. Instead of going out and trading with the one talent he had in order to at least gain more, he played it safe and dug a hole.

How many times do you play it safe rather than stepping out, being bold, and doing more? How many times do you neglect doing something above what is average just because no one instructed you to do anything extra? The master of these servants didn't necessarily tell them to go out and do more than what was required, but two of the servants went the extra mile just because average wasn't good enough.

When I heard this story, I had to ask myself if I was a one talent type of man. The one talent guy's mind-set was "I will not go above and beyond the call of duty simply because nobody instructed me to." He thought he was doing a good thing by just doing the bare minimum, while the other two guys decided to do what was outside of the normal expectations and increased tremendously.

There are times in life when doing only what is required will keep you at a level to only receive that which is standard. I tell myself this over and over all the time, "If you ever want to live outside of the ordinary, then act that way." It is impossible to become extraordinary until you do something outside of the ordinary. Author Tommy Newberry said: "Success is not an accident." He goes on to say, "If you want to lead an extraordinary life, find out what the ordinary do – and don't do it."

At the moment this information was revealed to me, I became a five talent man which meant I would never do just the minimum anymore. The problem was not my dead end job; the problem was how I performed and did the minimum just to get by at that job. I was no different than everyone else in my department. I came to work daily only doing what was required and not giving the people in authority any reason to see me differently from the crowd. Nothing about what I displayed demanded that I be given more or that I was deserving of something greater. Do your actions demand that you be rewarded on a greater scale than the average person?

Before learning this information, my attitude was to only do what my job description required. Even if it was something I could handle easily, my attitude was if it is not what they pay me for then I don't do it. Have you ever been around people that have this attitude about their profession? I can't tell you how many times I've been in a crowded store where the checkout lines are backed up into the aisles. There are always a few employees standing around and instead of volunteering to open a register or figure out how to assist in the chaotic situation, their mentality is they don't pay me to work the register. So they just look around aimlessly and only do exactly what is asked of them and not anything more. Take it from me, you will never prosper with that mind-set. In fact, that way of thinking will eventually demote and strip you from the little you currently have.

The one talent man was not only scolded by his master, but stripped of the one talent he was unfaithful over, and the one talent that he possessed was given to the five talent man. The five talent man had proven that he was willing to take what is and make it better, therefore being of greater value to his master. Sometimes you have to ask yourself how valuable are you to the company that you work for? That type of man who goes above and beyond will always be trusted with more. On the other hand, the one talent man was categorized as lazy because he only did just enough and in the end was left with absolutely nothing.

Is this your current way of thinking, and are you willing to change? Do you only do just enough in life and wonder why you always have just enough to get by? Those two things are connected. A "just enough" effort will only produce just enough results. Being honest with myself at that time, I knew this was one of the reasons I was not excelling. I had to make a decision and be willing to make a serious change. "You cannot expect to achieve new goals or move beyond your present circumstances unless you change." Motivational speaker and author Les Brown definitely has a way with words, but that was the quote that summed it up for me and forced me to do what was necessary to go higher in life.

Human nature craves and desires accomplishment. The essence of achieving is hard wired into our core, but are you willing to go through the process, change, and adapt to a new way of thinking in order to get there? The legendary NFL coach Vince Lombardi says: "The difference between a successful person and others is not a lack of strength, not a lack of knowledge, but rather a lack of will." Be willing to make the necessary adjustments to get the best life has to offer.

From that day on I paid attention to the small things, did what the one talent man wouldn't do, and very soon promotion came my way. It's the small adjustments in life that will push you ahead. It was a Tuesday afternoon around 3:30 p.m. when my entire department was called into a meeting and the supervisor told us that the department had been outsourced to another company. In other words, we all had been let go from the job. The word outsourced, downsized, or corporate restructure are just fancy terms for "You're fired." In my heart, I didn't understand because I had started giving my all at work. I was open to working late, weekends, and even holidays. I would do leftover work that other people should have been responsible for and not even gripe about it. I knew I had become the five talent man; bringing more to the table than what the job required. After hearing the news of being outsourced, my thought was this five talent man thing isn't working for me. As we walked out of the meeting room, everyone with sad looks on their faces, the supervisor touched me on the shoulder and said, "Hodges, let me speak with you for a minute. He pulled me to the side and what he told me literally changed everything. Mr. Haynes added, "We truly appreciate all your hard work and dedication to this company and you are an asset here. I apologize that the department is being outsourced but I'm sure we can find you another position here at the company." In pure shock and amazement, I only managed to reply, "You can find me another position here?" Mr. Haynes then informed me that in fact there were two positions in other departments that he felt I would be perfect for. He went on to say both of the other positions would mean a huge advancement for me with the company, and a tremendous raise in pay. I could hardly contain my excitement as this man almost begged me to stay with the company and consider taking one of the other positions that were available. Going above and beyond had shown them how valuable I was to their business, and when you are an asset to anyone or anything then your worth has just gone up.

As I walked out of the boardroom with the biggest smile ever on my face, Mr. Haynes said to me, "Hodges, please don't mention our conversation to any of the other employees in the department because I don't have a position for any of them, just you." I felt exactly how the five talent man must have felt when he was called good and faithful and allowed to be put in charge of much more. When you are faithful over the few, consequently you will become a ruler over the much.

I had learned a valuable lesson that applied not only to that job, but life in general. The way you get ahead is by going above and beyond. It is that intangible detail that will set you apart and promote you even in the midst of what seems to be difficult times. Put yourself in a position where your efforts will have to be noticed, and your worth valued at a much higher level. Doing just what is expected will never allow you to stand out among the crowd. The attitude to have is not to settle at good, strive to be great. If you have a choice between good and great, knowing that great is an option why would you ever settle for just being good?

It really doesn't matter if it's a job you are temporarily working at just to pay the bills or the business you are passionate about, give it your all. Dr. Martin Luther King, Jr. used to say: "Whatever your life's work is, do it well. A man should do his job so well that the living, the dead, and the unborn could do it no better."

Average should never be an option. Excellence is the only mentality a winner should have. To be just average is for the person only focusing on surviving to the next day. The excellence of who you are as a person should shine through no matter what you are doing. It doesn't matter if you are washing your spouse's car just to be nice, don't do it halfway. Do it so well that you "wow" that person and trust me, there will be a reward for you. My personal goal is to always wow a person when they encounter me or my company. It could be as simple as putting on a webinar or doing business during a conference call, but my mind always asks: how can I make this better? What can we do that is above and beyond to the point that no other company would even consider doing? What could I do that no one else would think to do concerning a conference call or webinar that would make it that much better? What would give my participants that wow factor? How can I under-promise and always over-deliver on everything I do?

A key to your success in life is to think and strategize in that way. Every move you plan to make, think about what else you can do just to gain an edge. Maybe you are a student in school writing a research paper - don't just write the paper as the professor asked and simply turn it in. Everyone else will do just that, so what makes your paper stand out? What makes your paper great rather than good? Instead of just turning your paper in as required, perhaps you take the extra time to go find a nice folder to present it in. To take an extra step to go get it printed on some nice textured type paper. Whatever it is, go beyond the call of duty and watch what happens next. If you are only doing what is expected or what someone instructed, that is not enough for greatness. The one way to always be average is to do just enough to get by. There is very little chance at excelling when the mentality is to do the bare minimum.

Ever had a job where you did just enough not to get fired? If you can't admit it, I can. How will you move to a higher level if you are not willing to do what the higher level requires? Here is the shift in mind-set– whatever is expected of you, find a way to do more. Stretch yourself to start doing things that you wouldn't normally do. If you do, I can promise a reward will be in your future. Where are you right now? How do you make that situation work better for you? Is your mind turning right now about the ways to go above and beyond? This principle will work not only in your professional life but also in your personal life. Apply it daily, and watch the amazing results.

THE THOUGHT PROCESS:

What came to mind as you read about going above and beyond?

Chapter 18

WINNING THE GAME!

"This is not the end, this is not even the beginning of the end, this is just perhaps the end of the beginning."

~ Winston Churchill

Fulfillment is something that is universal no matter what the goal or quest might be. Go to the ends of the earth and all people generally have the same motive for whatever they are doing. That motive is to get the best out of life and live it to the fullness of measure. We all may go about this in different ways and from different aspects of thought, but the motivation remains the same. We all may even have different definitions of what fulfillment means to us, but we all crave some level of satisfaction in our lives.

As human beings, we all desire to be happy and live a life that is rewarding in every possible way. Whether we consciously admit that or not, it is an unconscious desire that we all have. Along the journey we pick up certain things that are either helpful or very detrimental to the type of fulfillment we end up receiving in life. The various roadblocks, trials, tribulations, teachings, and certain experiences all play a role in how things turn out. Often, the more things we go through will cause us to stop pushing quite as hard for the true fulfillment we seek. There are situations in life that can abuse you so bad that fulfillment becomes something you only daydream about, and mere peace is what we settle for. There is nothing wrong with peace, please let me clarify that. However, it is possible to have peace without being truly fulfilled.

I remember my first little apartment with no furniture in it. True enough, I was at peace because I was thankful to at least have that tiny apartment. After all, it could have been worse. Even though I was at peace, it was not fulfilling for me because I never planned on staying in a 700 square foot empty apartment forever. My thoughts of fulfillment went a bit beyond that. During that time I arrived at a very profound destination of thought because I learned that even though peace is good, it's our choice to either stay there or move beyond that point to fulfillment. Either you accept peace as the best life has to offer, or decide to push yourself into a realm of endless possibilities. Sometimes we reach a level of peace and even though things may be better than they were in the past, we settle and believe that is as good as it gets.

Why do we put limits on our level of fulfillment? At what point did we start to believe and adopt the limitations that outside influences may have set? Limitations only exist within your mental scope of what you can fathom. That is the main reason this book deals so much with how you think. Author Joanna Russ said: "The trouble with men is that they have limited minds. That's the trouble with women, too." Once you take those limitations off, fulfillment will not only be possible but it will seem like the norm for your life.

We start out as children with dreams to conquer the world, and a belief system that says anything is possible. As a child, our faith has not yet been tainted with doubt and society's rationale. Therefore as a child, we are free to imagine and believe that anything is possible without limitation. However, as we start to grow up a negative change begins to occur. Somewhere between high school and college, between childhood and adulthood, our beliefs in the possibilities begin to diminish. Of course, we don't recognize this is happening at the time. It happens gradually and in a very subtle way. We simply say that those dreams we had when we were younger were just childish thoughts.

It is considered proper as an adult to tailor your dreams and goals so that they are more responsible and realistic. Those childhood thoughts of winning big turn into mere hopes of making sure the bills are paid each month and surviving through each day. We grow into adults that simply want to stay under the radar and maintain an easy level of being with no hassles. The thought of taking huge risks are often in the back of our minds, but our circumstances tell us now is not a good time. Stepping out into something new always sounds like a good idea, but oftentimes the reality of where we are pulls us back in to accept the mundane cycle.

What happens to us over time as we grow up? What does society and its way of thinking do to our spirit of triumph and victory? At what point do you start believing that sitting on the beaches of the world profiting from your passion is impossible? When did you accept and buy into this cubicle lifestyle with Mr. Johnson's bad breath constantly asking when the next report will be done? At what point in life did you say this is all life has to offer? What circumstances or situations in life caused you to conform to being a survivor and push away the thought of winning big? Who taught you that your wildest, most exciting dreams could not become reality? Or at what point did you start to believe that dreams were for unrealistic people, and responsible adults should only seek secure stability? One of the most accomplished women of our time, Oprah Winfrey, told us that: "The biggest adventure you can take is to live the life of your dreams." When did we dismiss that thought?

I ask all these questions because again, this book is designed to provoke deep thought about who you are and where you are, as well as to incite thoughts of why you are where you are. Take a moment to think about that, I know that was a lot of who, what, where, and why in one sentence. Please don't misunderstand the point here because the suggestion is not that you are currently in a bad place. I just want you to think about where you are and figure out if you got there because of unlimited thoughts or realistic suggestions. Are you in a good space or a great space? If it is only good, what would make it great? Remember the message behind the message, and the perspective it is coming from. What exactly are your thoughts saying to you? Are you getting answers to those questions in your mind, or wondering at what point you let go of the very thing you had a real passion for.

This level of thought is meant to generate awareness of what tomorrow will be like if you remain the same, or how tomorrow will be different if you decide to make certain adjustments. If you take nothing else from this book, understand that we are truly the captains of our own ship and we design our own destiny. I love what the English Poet William Ernest Henley said in the last two lines of his great poem: "I am the master of my fate; I am the captain of my soul." Unfortunately we live in a society that forces its limitations on us daily, so as you get older it takes more work to think outside of that box. It takes a great deal of diligent effort to remind yourself that there truly are no limitations, and you are free to design the destiny you desire.

To get to this point, it becomes an act of reprogramming yourself to get all those limiting ways of thinking out of your system. As a kid it's so easy because we don't have parameters set just yet. Kids will touch a hot stove just to see what will happen and even if its burns them, they are still fascinated about the possibilities of what that stove can accomplish. Guess what? Instead of being afraid of it, most kids will go back a second time and touch the stove again. That level of curiosity without fear in order to reach beyond the boundaries and see what may be possible, is priceless. It's not until some adult conditions them to the dangers of the stove that they create a fear for it and stop going near it.

Now while educating a child on the dangers of a stove has it benefits, we do this in all other areas of their lives as well. Each of us as adults has been conditioned in this way. We start out with endless ideas of what we will do when we grow up and what we will become. That all sounds great until some adult, television, internet, or the messages that society puts forth help create fear and a sense of not pursuing our desires. It is the art of society helping to shape our parameters by telling us what is possible and what is not. It's like putting an invisible fence around the mind of a person so that whenever they travel outside of that fence an alarm goes off and sounds a danger signal, which confines them within the boundaries of the fence.

I think back to my childhood and those times in school when the teacher would ask what you wanted to be when you grow up. Do you remember the amazing, outside of the box answers that some students came up with? Now when you are really young, let's say first or second grade, and asked that question, the answers are so big and miraculous that we can hardly fathom those things as adults today. At that age, kids will tell you they want to be an astronaut or the most famous person in the world. Some kids will even say things like I want to be a doctor and cure cancer because one of their family members died of the disease. At that moment in a child's life, he or she believes with all their heart they can do whatever they say and in their mind, it's not even a difficult task to accomplish.

Often a teacher or an adult will just laugh at a child's reply to a question like that. The teacher laughs because as an adult he/she already has parameters in place and doesn't truly believe what that child is saying is possible. As adults we are conditioned to believe that those huge outside of the box ideas just don't happen, at least not for everyone. We believe that if those big dreams or goals do happen, it will only happen for a rare few. The reason adults laugh when children speak is because we remember that level of optimism before we became realistic and practical. So most of the time as adults with our broken mentality, we feel it is our job to help a child shape their dreams into something we feel would be achievable. Consciously we may not think or even understand and realize that is what we are doing, but it is normal for us to teach and create boundaries because we have them in our own lives. That is such a tragic thing to do to a child, but it was done to us and we genuinely feel it is the right thing to do. Sooner or later the teacher or adult in a child's life will impose their fears on that child.

Three to five years later if you ask the same child what they want to be when they grow up, their answers will start to become more and more "realistic." Give that some serious thought, because it's an absolutely twisted concept and we continue to do it over and over again by conforming people to boxes of what we believe, or have been taught is safe and possible. Take that same child when they get to high school, and they may still have huge dreams but they aren't nearly as radical as they were in first or second grade.

This process is called conditioning. To us as adults we say it's great because the child has grown up and now they have real goals that can be accomplished. The fact that our fear has diminished their vision down to what we consider safe is not what I would call an accomplishment. The same child in high school may still want to become a doctor, but at that point boundaries have been set in their mind. The dream or goal of curing cancer isn't the main focus anymore. The level of fear and thoughts of impossibility says just becoming a doctor is hard enough, so curing cancer is out of the question. After all, at that point the young person understands that no one has ever cured cancer and rationale says if that is the case, it's very unlikely that they would be able to do something no one else has done. Then once that same child enters college and learns how long it takes to become a doctor and all the requirements involved, learning the medical school dropout rate statistics, and all of the people that didn't make it, becoming a receptionist in a doctor's office doesn't sound half bad.

Now I'm being crass with my examples here just to make a dramatic point. Life isn't about the huge accomplishment that society recognizes. Please don't misinterpret the example here and miss the main point. It doesn't matter if you are a doctor or the person that makes sure the office is clean. The status of where you are in life means nothing in comparison to what I am talking about. Also a person's status in life doesn't always guarantee or equal fulfillment. The type of winning I have been referring to throughout this entire book has absolutely nothing to do with fancy titles, wealth, or material possessions. The level of winning I am talking about is true inner fulfillment regarding the things you desire and how to create them at will. How to turn everything in your mind that makes you smile, gives you joy, or a sense of purpose into a tangible reality.

The point I want to make with the example is, are you truly where you desire to be? Have you or are you creating what is in your heart? Or are you in a place just because it's peaceful and comfortable? Is life a joy or just a chore that you dread daily? Is your life today in a certain place because it seemed more practical? The goal you are going after, is it really what you originally had in mind? Or is the goal just more realistic according to the boundaries that have been placed on you? Those are very critical questions that you have to pose to yourself and answer honestly for your own personal development.

It could very well be that the conditioning of life did not grab a hold of you and today the fulfillment you desire is a reality. To you I say congratulations, but your job is not yet done. If you are at that level, then it's your responsibility to help others reach that same level of fulfillment. Think about the joy you have because the success in your life is not just about wealth or doing great business. Think about how great it feels to know you live a life that is purpose driven. Doesn't everyone in the world deserve that feeling? True fulfillment is accomplished when all areas of life are thriving at the same time. That is the reason you have to have a personal foundation, so that you can professionally achieve. The professional success means so much more when it has other areas of success in your life that it can hang out with so to speak.

Personally, you will have great fulfillment when you know how to cultivate great relationships which can make or break you as far as real happiness is concerned. Spiritually, you are fulfilled when you can walk a path where a level of soundness has taken place and you are aware and confident in what you believe. Then health wise, fulfillment comes when you are conscious and living a lifestyle that promotes good health and physically you feel great. If your focus becomes to get all those areas to work together at the same time, then that is winning in life and not just merely existing from day-to-day.

If that is your experience then it is worth sharing with others so they understand the possibilities. If that is not your experience yet, then no worries because you are now on the path to making the adjustments necessary to create the life you want. The key is to create the life you envision, not the life society has deemed successful. Will there be obstacles? Yes. Will there be times you feel like just giving up? Absolutely. In those moments just remind yourself to take just one more step, move one more inch, and the reward you will receive will make the fight worth it. "Success is not measured by what you accomplish, but by the opposition you have encountered, and the courage with which you have maintained the struggle against overwhelming odds." Author Orison Swett Marden said that, and I would have to agree wholeheartedly. So, there will be some fights in this life and some opposition, but you were born equipped with all you need to overcome and conquer. Remember, it's not the things outside of you that will help you win; it is the things inside of you that will give you all the tools you need to achieve.

Look deep within yourself and think, strategize, and plan your way through this life. Make every move of your chess game count. Always remember that winners never, ever quit. You may take a minute to catch your breath and readjust, but quitting is never an option. There is a great saying that has become the slogan at my empowerment company and I give it to you now to repeat to yourself as often as you like. It's a game changer because it will set your mind to where it always needs to be.

The slogan simply says: "Winning is not just an option – It's simply a way of life."

THE THOUGHT PROCESS:

What is true fulfillment for you?

CPSIA information can be obtained
at www.ICGtesting.com
Printed in the USA
FFOW01n1642090116
20283FF